Intergenerational Catechesis

Intergenerational Catechesis

Revitalizing Faith through African-American Storytelling

timone a davis

LEXINGTON BOOKS
Lanham • Boulder • New York • London

Published by Lexington Books
An imprint of The Rowman & Littlefield Publishing Group, Inc.
4501 Forbes Boulevard, Suite 200, Lanham, Maryland 20706
www.rowman.com

6 Tinworth Street, LondonSE11 5AL, United Kingdom

British Library Cataloguing in Publication Information Available

Library of Congress Control Number: 2020952580

ISBN 9781498595940 (cloth) I ISBN 9781498595964 (pbk) I ISBN 9781498595957 (epub)

Contents

Acknowledgments

"We've Come This Far by Faith" is a gospel song by Carlton Pearson that captures what I am feeling at this moment. I have wanted to write a book for over twenty years, but I just didn't have the discipline to sit down and write. Some call it writer's block, but that's not true. I didn't have faith. I didn't have faith in myself nor did I have faith in God. But God had faith in me. In small ways, God kept telling me I could write. And slowly those words seeped into my spirit. This book captures my life's work, sharing the good news of what God has done, is doing, and will do.

When I think about all the people who I want to lift up, I am filled with images of people who have poked and prodded me, picked me up when I fell, nurtured me when I couldn't see my way, challenged me to reach deeper into my being. This attempt at acknowledging them all will surely fall short as I am only naming a few people in my most recent past. My mother, Gaynell Burrell, has taught me so much about love especially as dementia has taken over her mind. Through the loss of her brilliant mind, I have arrived at a better understanding of unconditional love—it challenges, it leaps, it dives, it questions but it doesn't stop loving. This has helped me open myself more fully to transformations that come when patience wears thin.

I wonder if this book would have gotten written if it wasn't for the requirement to write a book for tenure at the Institute of Pastoral Studies (IPS) at Loyola University Chicago. The tenure journey has helped me see God's action not just in my preaching but also in my academic writing. While I have been privileged to share my catechetical ideas with students at IPS, I am especially grateful to Timothy Goldston, Ifeyinwa Exeoke, and Tiberth Hagos—students in my course *My Story-Your Story: A Pastoral Response for 21st Century Catechesis*—at the Institute for Black Catholic Studies at the

Xavier University of Louisiana in 2019. Those three students pushed me to articulate African-American storytelling for those unfamiliar with it.

When the deadline became an "object in mirror is closer than it appears," I turned to the Cistercian monks of Mepkin Abbey in Moncks Corner, South Carolina, for a place of solitude and prayer in order to write. Pausing for prayer throughout the day opened me to God in new ways. If you happen by Mepkin Abbey, stop in for prayer. Your spirit will thank you.

My husband, Orlando Davis, asked me way too many times, "Are you done?" His constant question, while annoying, also encouraged me to finish. Cayden Davis-Polk, my grandson, provided exactly what I needed when I was too tired to go on—new life, wonder, and awe. Just as I neared the end, administrative tasks were my undoing. Nephtalie Lesperance, the IPS research assistant, stepped right up and took care of things. Her calm demeanor and expertise are immeasurable.

As I write this, I am aware that I have only begun to name the numerous people who have prayed for me and whispered words of encouragement— "We've Come This Far by Faith."

Introduction

Once Upon a Time

Stories are Beings. You invite them to live with you. They'll teach you what they know in return for being a good host. When they're ready to move on they'll let you know.
Then you pass them on to someone else.

—Cree Storyteller[1]

Once upon a time, in lands far and near, people attended church every week. Many people even attended church daily. Others would gather in churches for bible studies, prayer meetings, book clubs, baptisms, religious education, weddings, and funerals. And then, no one gathered in churches. Worship in churches stopped. Bible studies stopped. Religious education came to a screeching halt. There were no baptisms or weddings, and funerals were limited to ten people. This phenomenon caught many by surprise, sending their spiritual well-being into shock. When I received a text from my pastor saying my presentation was canceled because the church was closed, I thought it was a joke. When I inquired, he said, all Masses have been canceled due to the virus. "What?!?! Who cancels Mass? Who closes churches?" Severe acute respiratory syndrome coronavirus 2 (SARS-CoV-2)/coronavirus disease (COVID-19)[2] has caused us to close many things. In lands far and near, people have been told to stay at home, to shelter in place, and to leave their homes only to acquire essential things like food. Worship and religious education were not considered essential. What does it mean to believers who have gathered for years and those just beginning to learn that attending church is not essential? I cannot answer this question. What I do know is that people will be looking to share their experiences of this time and searching for ways to process the effects COVID-19 has had on them and others, far

1

and near. Stories will be told. This book can assist in the storytelling process as it seeks to reimagine catechesis. It provides a way to re-member what it's like to be with others after months of social distancing. It asks that we look inward to see outward.

Yesterday, when attending Mass was ordinary, people entered the Catholic faith via the Rite of Christian Initiation of Adults (RCIA) process that journeys with adults who desire to enter the Catholic Church. This process of entry into the Church had me looking at my own faith and what I found lacking. As a process within catechesis, or religious education as some call it, RCIA had me looking at evangelization differently. I thought that if we helped people better understand the Catholic faith and its intricacies, people would become more active in their faith lives and the Church would have a stronger presence in our living—our decision-making. I took this early thinking into high school theology classrooms in 1998 before moving on to Reclaiming Christ in Life (ReCiL), an archdiocesan young adult ministry in 2004. It was in working with young adults that I discovered how little information was available to address their needs. A great deal of information is available for Catholic youth in the United States, but once these youth turn eighteen, youth groups and many other forms of programming trickles to almost nothing. Of course there are young adult ministries and groups around the United States; however, these are exceptions and not the rule.[3] From RCIA I took its focus on persons becoming community and expanded on how people develop community—they tell stories. By sharing how they came to be engaged in the RCIA process, people were telling stories. The emphasis of ReCiL is on small faith-based communities creating "sacred space" in which to speak freely about God and the Church in their lives. Storytelling figures prominently in this process by helping young adults to speak freely about their issues, circumstances, and sexuality for example, with regard to the Church, parents, friends, and the community. I have since learned that storytelling helps not only young adults but all of us to make sense of life.

What happens in the story exchange process is the discovery of connections—connections we so desperately need. By focusing on the connections, *My Story-Your Story*, a way of doing African-American storytelling, emerges as a method of catechesis, which helps people live the gospel. It will be the primary method of doing intergenerational catechesis.

As an African-American laywoman in the Catholic Church, it is often difficult to give voice to the issues and stresses one faces in life and in the Church. African-American storytelling has helped me find my voice and better understand my journey and its relationship to the Catholic Christian story. Through story, one is able to better connect to the content and context: teachings, morals, values, culture, and ethnicity of her/his life. Story is the way we will grow stronger while dealing with the effects of COVID-19. "Story is a powerful part of human existence. We humans live an evolving narrative, or story, that forms from the storied world around us."[4]

This book seeks to retrieve the forgotten practice of African-American storytelling that once served not just as entertainment but aided the community in recording and sharing history and put it in dialogue with intergenerational catechesis, a more holistic understanding of the Catholic faith. This research will explore the use of story in catechesis, show how the African-American tradition of storytelling addresses the particular needs of multiple generations, and assists them to better understand themselves in relation to God and others. For "the Gospel seeks a catechesis which is open, generous and courageous in reaching people where they live, especially in encountering those nuclei in which the most elementary and fundamental cultural exchanges take place, such as the family, the school, the work environment and free time."[5]

In particular, this book seeks to establish the role storytelling plays in revitalizing people's faith.

The Catholic faith sustains the oral tradition of the Scriptures, both Hebrew (Old) and New Testament. African-American storytelling draws upon the oral tradition of peoples of Africa in order to share stories of our ancestors, both biblical and familial. This method of sharing beliefs will be explored in this book. I am engaging the hermeneutics of Black Catholic theology proposed by M. Shawn Copeland and pastoral theology by Emmanual Lartey. Beginning with an understanding that Black theology arises from a despised Black identity, Copeland states that "black theology carries within it the seed of universal concern that extends most particularly to all marginalized and oppressed persons and . . . advocates for the liberation of all—oppressed as well as oppressor."[6] This is important now that many find themselves marginalized and oppressed by COVID-19. Lartey's focus in pastoral theology is one of engagement, a "way of being and doing."[7] His highlighting of experience, context, and tradition helps me bring narrative to the forefront where real-life experiences can be taken into consideration.

This research is for catechists, religious education teachers, adult faith formation directors, campus ministers, pastoral associates, pastors and anyone else interested in using story in faith formation, religious education and for spiritual growth. Though in a Catholic setting, this work may have portability for other denominations seeking to enhance their religious education and/or faith formation.

There are several terms used in this book that require explanation for their use. The first term is *My Story-Your Story*. The linkage of *My Story-Your Story* speaks to the connection I believe exists between persons that make us a community. *My Story-Your Story* strengthens that connection as each person begins to see her/his own life as part of a whole, as part of a community. *My Story-Your Story* is about our connections, our relationships, and how they encourage us to grow. My story reveals God in my life and in doing so invites you to reveal God in yours. "Go back and tell people of the great things that God has done for you, for your story is for others and, once they have it, they can do what is necessary for them. It is no longer just yours."[8]

The next term is *African-American*. When speaking of African-American, one will find a variety of meanings, since the naming of the people who descended from African slaves in the United States has gone through many stages. These names reflect the struggle for "self-identification and collective consciousness. . . . Regardless of what we call ourselves, in order to be authentic we need to be aware that we are an African people."[9] This understanding of naming serves as the foundation on which I put Diana L. Hayes's definition of African-American that I will be using for this work: "Those Black Americans whose origins date from the period of slavery in the United States whether their ancestors were slave or free."[10] Though the term is not always hyphenated, I am hyphenating African-American to denote the linkage of a heritage that is lost and cannot readily be retrieved.

I use the term kin-dom in place of kingdom to be more inclusive. It calls to mind our union, our family status, in God. The final term is *catechesis*. "The word catechesis comes from the Greek verb *katéchein*, which means 'to resound,' 'to echo,' or 'to hand down.' Thus, the etymology of the word implies an oral instruction."[11] Given that catechesis is an "oral reechoing," we understand that story provides meaning to our living. It is the narrative that explains our living and our circumstances.

In chapter 1, I include an understanding of the five generations alive today before discussing culture and context, the effects of technology, and the influence of the hip-hop culture. The Millennial generation is the discussion partner in these sections. In chapter 2, I explore the history and practice of African-American storytelling beginning with the African oral tradition. I explore the relationship between African-American storytelling and faith and the role of scripture. I look at the various ways African-American storytelling is used to shape people and discuss how African-American storytelling can be liberating. Chapter 3 addresses the role of faith formation in the lives of the Catholic faithful and how theological reflection is a key component. I explore the relationship between catechesis and evangelization, and I describe the connection of *My Story-Your Story* to the Christian story. In chapter 4, I explore intergenerational and historical trauma and their effect on memory which then calls for a healing of memory that enables people to tell their own story. The final chapter, chapter 5, provides strategies for using African-American storytelling on personal, parish, and diocesan levels.

NOTES

1. Megan McKenna and Tony Cowan, *Keepers of the Story* (Maryknoll, NY: Orbis Press, 1997), 45.

2. World Health Organization, "Naming the Coronavirus Disease (COVID-19) and the Virus that Causes It," accessed March 19, 2020, https://www.who.int/emergencies/diseases/novel-coronavirus-2019/technical-guidance/naming-the-coronavirus-disease-(covid-2019)-and-the-virus-that-causes-it.

3. Mike Hayes, *Googling God: The Religious Landscape of People in their 20s and 30s* (New York/Mahwah, NJ: Paulist Press, 2007), 25.

4. Anne E. Streaty Wimberley, *Soul Stories: African American Christian Education* (Nashville, TN: Abingdon Press, 2005), 3.

5. Congregation for the Clergy, *General Directory for Catechesis* (Washington, DC: United States Catholic Conference, 1997), 211. Subsequent references will be made parenthetically citing *GDC*.

6. M. Shawn Copeland, "Method in Emerging Black Catholic Theology," in *Taking Down Our Harps: Black Catholics in the United States*, eds. Diana L. Hayes and Cyprian Davis (Maryknoll, NY: Orbis Books, 1998), 124.

7. Emmanuel Lartey, "Practical Theology as Theological Form," in *The Blackwell Reader in Pastoral and Practical Theology*, eds. James Woodward and Stephen Pattison (Malden, MA: Blackwell, 2000), 131.

8. McKenna and Cowan, 188.

9. J. Deotis Roberts, *Africentric Christianity: A Theological Appraisal for Ministry* (Valley Forge: Judson Press, 2000), 11–12.

10. Diana L. Hayes, *And Still We Rise: An Introduction to Black Liberation Theology* (New York/Mahwah, NJ: Paulist Press, 1996), 6.

11. Thomas H. Groome, *Christian Religious Education: Sharing Our Story and Vision* (San Francisco: Harper and Row, 1981. Reprint, San Francisco: Jossey-Bass, 1999), 26.

Chapter 1

The Church

Who Are We?

In the Catholic Church, pastors, pastoral ministers, catechists, vocation directors, and others are questioning how to better engage people in their Catholic faith: liturgy, sacramental celebrations, ministry, Church leadership, vocations, devotions, and education. Of the many questions asked: "How do we strengthen vocations?" "How do we encourage young adults to take leadership roles in the Church?" "Why can't women be ordained deacons?" "How do we stop young people from leaving the Church?" "What do we want from the Church?" I address one, "Who are we?" To answer this question, I expound upon generational distinctions that make up the United States. In the first section, Generations of the Twenty-First Century, I explore significant U.S. cultural influences and events that have helped to shape each generation alive today: Traditionalists/Silent, Baby Boomers, Generation X, Millennials, and Generation Z. In the remaining sections—Culture and Context, Technology, Hip-Hop and Its Influence, Identity, and Spirituality/ Spiritual Awareness—I focus on Millennials. I am choosing to focus on Millennials because they are a generation of shapeshifters, moving in and through the various cultural changes and technological advancements to form a new understanding of church. Almost everyone wants to be an agent of change, but few think of change in terms of shapeshifting: altering the shape, reformatting the view, shifting the paradigm, modifying the program, reformatting the drive, renovating the room, and editing the text. In a world where materialism reigns supreme, and the gospel of prosperity is preached all around, Millennials challenge us by asking the questions we don't always want to answer, for example, "Why are you Catholic?" "What does it mean to be a Catholic today?" While many of us have not gotten beyond the "I've always been Catholic" answer, Millennial shapeshifters are no longer satisfied with this childhood understanding of Catholicism. They are calling the

Church to a real sense of faith formation, where solutions offer better ways to deal with this world.[1]

As you will see, there are many U.S. cultural influences affecting each generation. For this discussion I focus on two: technology and hip-hop. Narrative plays a significant role in both hip-hop and technology as each allows people new ways in which to express themselves. This analysis will show how people across generational, cultural, and contextual borders share an oral-aural quality of experience.

GENERATIONS OF THE TWENTY-FIRST CENTURY

The term generation[2] is fluid in its definition, referring not only to people but also to things, particularly electronic devices.[3] In reference to people, the definition has undergone a change.

> Until recently, a generation was defined the same way a genealogy was: by succession backwards from parents to grandparents to great grandparents, or ahead from parents to children to grandchildren. Each unit in that succession is a generation. . . . The baby boomer concept of generations is different. It suggests that people are largely defined by some major event or attribute that they have in common, even though their exact birth dates are different. This definition emphasizes the fact that people a few years apart in chronological age will have the same cultural outlook if they have been exposed at roughly the same formative time in their lives to something as major as war or a significant technological innovation.[4]

Generation, therefore, is "a group of individuals, most of whom are the same approximate age, having similar ideas, problems, attitudes, etc."[5] In a Pew Research Center report, generation is further defined to include

> three overlapping processes: (1) Life cycle effects: Young people may be different from older people today, but they may well become more like them tomorrow, once they themselves age. (2) Period effects: Major events (wars; social movements; economic downturns; medical, scientific or technological breakthroughs) affect all age groups simultaneously, but the degree of impact may differ according to where people are located in the life cycle. (3) Cohort effects: Period events and trends often leave a particularly deep impression on young adults because they are still developing their core values; these imprints stay with them as they move through their life cycle.[6]

David and Jonah Stillman say this about generations in the Foreword of Hayim Herring's book *Connecting Generations: Bridging the Boomer, Gen*

X, and Millennial Divide, "When many think of a generation, they immediately think of a person's age . . . contrary to popular belief, connections or conflicts between generations go much deeper. The key to understanding generations and why connections and conflicts arise is to adopt an ageless attitude. You do this by looking at how each generation shares a common history. Certain events and conditions have determined a lot about who we are and how we see the world. As a result of these events and conditions, each generation has adopted its own unique 'generational personality.' "[7] This fuller understanding of generation will allow me to better explain the role the U.S. culture continues to play in shaping people's lives.

I am including a brief look into postmodernity because "postmodernity . . . includes ways of life as well as forms of thinking . . . which can be viewed more as a 'sensibility.' "[8] These ways of life and forms of thinking connect with the understanding of generation as including the life cycle, period, and cohort effects that shape us today. Postmodernity "is [also] characterized by new sensitivities on three fronts: ecology, feminism and the return of spirituality."[9] This understanding of postmodernity is calling people back to care for all of creation, listening to the voices of women, and establishing and/ or maintaining a relationship with God. In thinking about the period effects mentioned above in regard to generation, we can see how "the very possibility of religious faith today is influenced by cultural factors. Our receptivity for revelation is more shaped by culture than by philosophical clarities. We seldom live by ideas or ideologies but rather by images of life communicated by our surrounding worlds. Hence the cultural wavelength is central for understanding the shifting currents within religious commitment now."[10] Within these shifting currents, I take up the discussion of generation distinctions. It should be noted that the birth year ranges used here are estimations depending on what source is consulted.[11]

Traditionalist/Silent

The Traditionalist/Silent generation[12] (born 1925–1945) came of age during World War II, the Korean War, the Great Depression, the New Deal, the Rise of corporations, and the rise of the Space Age. Their time of great poverty was followed by great prosperity. The Traditionalists/Silent generation trusted the government, respected authority, and believed in sacrificing for a greater good. They were hard workers—loyal to organizations/employers—with a dependability that focused on getting the job done. They had a strong sense of family, with multiple generations often living in the same household. They also believed that the hierarchical structure was to be respected and adhered to. The Church is seen as a place of refuge even as it changes dramatically (Vatican II). Their technological advances were the radio, mimeograph, rotary phones, and slide rules.

Baby Boomers

The Baby Boomers (born 1946–1963) came of age during the Cold and Vietnam Wars, Watergate, civil rights laws, the energy crisis, color television, and recreational sex. There was an overall atmosphere of distrust of the government and of authority. The United States at this time is undergoing economic growth and expansion of industry into other countries. White Catholics have integrated into the United States's dominant white Protestant social and political scene, altering that group's previously held views about them.[13] As children, they experienced a Church in transition, which led them to challenge many of the Church's teachings, especially those dealing with morality. "The morally-driven political struggles of the times—especially the civil rights movement and to a lesser degree the anti-Vietnam war movement—changed Catholic institutional and religious self-understanding. . . . The focus of Catholic attention on power, authority, equality, and discrimination in the public sphere invariably turned back on the Church itself. In time, many Catholic liberals adopted a rights-based language that raised the question of the rights of Catholics in the Church itself."[14] As a result, the Church for them is not seen as the place to go for refuge.

Generation X

Generation X (born 1964–1979) comes of age after abortion has been legalized, forcing the Catholic Church into the limelight on the issue as Catholic women take advantage of this option. As teens and young adults, Generation Xers are witnesses of televised war, microwave ovens, rap and grunge music, rising divorce rates, HIV/AIDS, personal home computers, home video games, the internet, and the fall of the Berlin Wall. As latchkey children, "school-aged children of working parents who must spend part of the day unsupervised (as at home),"[15] they have become adults who don't often look beyond themselves for support.

> The latchkey childhood of [Generation Xers] was central in establishing [their] deep relationship with popular culture—largely through the media. In loco parentis, television provided daily entertainment for those who had to fill time between the end of the school day and the return of working parents. . . . The importance of the latchkey experience in shaping [this] generation during its most malleable years can hardly be overstated. Massive amounts of unsupervised childhood time enabled [their] addiction to and indulgence in popular

culture. . . . This entry into the world of pop culture at such a young age is one reason [this] generation is unique.[16]

White Catholics at this time have largely become part of the middle class, "a fluid heterogeneous socioeconomic grouping composed principally of business and professional people, bureaucrats, and some farmers and skilled workers sharing common social characteristics and values."[17] This inclusion, coupled with a more ecumenical understanding of evangelization[18] in the Catholic Church, gave way to an acceptance of other Christian faiths, resulting in Generation Xers having little to no experience of anti-Catholicism. In the spirit of ecumenism, this generation was taught that they need to be responsible for their own faith journey while seeking out the commonalities among other Christian denominations.[19]

Millennials

Millennials (born 1980–1995) came of age in the midst of uncertain times. Their economy was unstable: major corporations went bankrupt, executives stole money from their employees using clever business strategies, long-time employees lost their jobs because of downsizing, home foreclosures rose, and jobs that fit their education and skill-set were and are hard to find. Manufacturing of U.S. goods is mostly done by other countries making it difficult to find non-skilled employment. Millennials are the first generation to witness a live attack on the country during peacetime (September 11, 2001). They are witnesses, victims, and survivors of new forms of U.S. violence: school shootings, workplace and shopping mall killings, increased child abuse and sexual assault, rising gang violence, and assaults on individuals because of their sexual orientation.

> They are growing up with mass murder and drugs in schools, entertained by violence and crime on television and film, increasingly aware of the lies they inherit from society, impatient with the political deceit and corruption of elected officials, misdirected by a capitalist culture, dying of AIDS, manipulated to back an unnecessary war in Iraq, and misinterpreted by [older] adults who exclude them from conversations about the future[.][20]

Alongside this uncertainty is the change in food production and consumption patterns (fast, genetically modified, and artificial food); rising medical costs; and declining healthcare coverage, especially for the poor and the elderly. With Millennials we see the rise in "spiritual, but not religious." The Pew Research Center states that "one-third of adults under 30 are religiously unaffiliated today, the highest percentages ever in Pew Research Center polling."[21]

Generation Z

Generation Z (born 1996–2012) is the most racially and ethnically diverse generation.[22] They are growing up with technology in a way that previous generations have not. They know color television with channels numbering into the hundreds, alongside on-demand video streaming, that is, Netflix, Amazon Prime, and hulu. "By the time they were in their teens, the primary means by which young Americans connected with the web was through mobile devices, WIFI and high-bandwidth cellular service. Social media, constant connectivity, and on-demand entertainment and communication are innovations Millennials adapted to as they came of age. For [Generation Z] these are largely assumed."[23] The clergy sexual abuse scandal that began to surface in the late 1980s is a mainstay in this generation—they do not know the Catholic Church apart from it. Generation Z is also coming of age in an era of "fake news." It is not clearly known where this generation's faith is as they watch Millennials leave and/or struggle to remain relevant within the Church. Though the implications of "fake news" and being "always on" for this generation are not yet known, I contend that now is a great moment for intergenerational catechesis as Generation Z looks for truth and ways to sustain themselves in times of trial and suffering.

This brief look inside the above-mentioned generations illustrates the early movement occurring within the Church where one's response to the Church and her teachings is a direct result of what is happening in U.S. dominant Protestant culture. In the following sections, I focus on Millennials (used interchangeably with young adults)—the population that is leaving the Church the fastest—to best illustrate the need for intergenerational catechesis and African-American storytelling.

CULTURE AND CONTEXT

In addition to looking at generational distinctions, we must also look at culture and context. Culture is the lens through which a person views everything; it is a way of being in the world; it is the context in which one lives; it is one's worldview shaped by origin, socioeconomics, race, religion (or lack of), and age. It is important because the person is important. What shapes a person also shapes his/her response/interaction with God. Linked to culture is context, the situation in which one lives. "As our cultural and historical context plays a part in the construction of the reality in which we live, so our context influences the understanding of God and the expression of faith."[24] In defining U.S. young adults, it is important to see that there exists a "secular" culture that is comprised of certain values, customs, and practices that shapes how young adults not only view themselves but also how they respond to issues of faith.[25] The Bradley Project on America's National Identity continues the discussion on culture:

> America is unique among nations in being founded not on a common ethnicity, but on a set of ideas. A nation founded on ethnicity perpetuates itself by the fact of birth. But a nation founded on an idea starts anew with each generation and with each new group of immigrants. Knowing what America stands for is not a genetic inheritance. It must be learned, both by the next generation and by those who come to this country. In this way, a nation founded on an idea is inherently fragile. And a nation that celebrates the many ways we are different from one another must remind itself constantly of what we all share.[26]

This view of America (the United States) helps clarify the need to look at generational differences as affected by society and Church.

> At one time there was an urgent concern for recognizing our differences, which allowed the contributions of minorities and immigrants to be fully told. But today there is also a yearning for national unity and common purpose, a desire to appreciate what is great about America, and not just to dwell on its past wrongs.[27]

The U.S. culture has largely influenced young adults through its media-heavy, electronic-laden society.

> [F]or Xers, popular culture is a major meaning-making system. Thus religious statements about the generation must take pop culture into account. For the young adult, many of life's most religious experiences happen outside religious institutions and "official" worship services. . . . Many are at arm's length from religious institutions. . . . At the same time [they] are nurtured by the amniotic fluid of popular culture with the media as a primary source of meaning. . . . A generation on such intimate terms with popular culture is bound to practice religion at least partly in and through this medium. [They] express [their] religious interests, dreams, fear, hopes, and desires through popular culture.[28]

This understanding of Generation X helps us better understand how

> [t]echnological change and generational change often go hand in hand. That's certainly the story of the Millennials and their embrace of all things digital. The internet and mobile phones have been broadly adopted in America in the past 15 years, and Millennials have been leading technology enthusiasts. For them, these innovations provide more than a bottomless source of information and

entertainment, and more than a new ecosystem for their social lives. They also are a badge of generational identity.[29]

This generation, therefore, is "dealing with new problems, in the North American setting: high expectations for material success; constant market-place pressures to buy commodities and be commodities; highly sexualized world and social interactions; high expectation of their own maturity and independence."[30] Amid these high expectations, young adults feel the pressures of being the best as defined by music videos, the latest gym shoe design, or hairstyle, often competing for and accumulating things that don't really interest them. "Contemporary American [young adults] have emerged as the most brand-oriented, consumer-involved, and materialistic generation in history."[31] "In comparison to baby boomers, [Millennials] have earlier exposure to and more involvement with adult worlds."[32] Yet this exposure and involvement does not translate so easily to matters of faith. Clearly, "[m]arket pressures are having a dramatic effect, not just economically, but emotionally on the lives of [young adults]."[33] With this in mind, I want to address the fact that there exists in the United States, a culture/context that affects young adults, no matter their ethnicity, social status, and education, because "[t]he United States is the most consumer-oriented society in the world."[34]

This consumer-oriented society has directly affected young adults' view of faith and the Catholic Church. "Consumer culture forms people in consumerist habits of use and interpretation, which believers, in turn, bring to their religious beliefs and practice. Thus, while theology can offer daring and radical counternarratives by drawing on the rich wisdom of religious traditions, these responses are subject to the same fate as other cultural objects within consumer culture."[35] With a consumer mentality, Catholic young adults "shop" through Catholic Church teachings, trying on and discarding the ones they don't like or are ill-fitting.

> [T]he real problem [then] with consumer culture lies in the structures and practices that systematically confuse and misdirect well-intentioned people seeking to do good things such as show solidarity with others, find spiritual transformation, and practice their sincerely held religious beliefs. . . . When consumption becomes the dominant cultural practice, belief is systematically misdirected from traditional religious practices into consumption.[36]

With a focus on material possessions many young adults find themselves quickly in debt, and the efforts to work to pay the debt can be hampered by reduced work hours or high turnover rate or the instability of employers. Those who cannot find employment may seek other ways to obtain the "things" they are convinced they must have. "The [Millennial] generation is particularly susceptible to high rates of job turnover that are associated with broader trends in the economy, such as rapid technological change, greater use of outsourcing, and high rates of business failure."[37] Since this discussion of culture and context is directly influenced by technology, a brief discussion on that topic follows this section.

TECHNOLOGY

Technological advancements and their availability have grown so rapidly that many don't see themselves separate from it. As Millennials adjusted to being "always on," Generation Z

> are history's first "always connected" generation. Steeped in digital technology and social media, they treat their multi-tasking hand-held gadgets almost like a body part—for better and worse. More than eight-in-ten say they sleep with a cell phone glowing by the bed, poised to disgorge texts, phone calls, e-mails, songs, news, videos, games and wake-up jingles."[38]

The internet has opened the door to e-mail, file sharing, instant messaging, and instant access to information, locally and globally. Personal computers/ laptops with WIFI make the internet readily available almost anywhere. Cell phones with video, camera, music, e-mail, and texting abilities allow young adults to keep their fingers on the pulse of "now." This type of availability to information lends itself to the belief that all aspects of life, even faith, can function this way. "We need always to assume that a large percentage of young adults believe that instant gratification is merely a click of a mouse or a touch of a button away and that they can apply this to every area of their life, religion included."[39] Being connected/plugged in/turned on most of the time allows young adults to be bombarded with images and sounds that force them to "become passive filters of the flood of data streaming toward [them]."[40] As passive filters, they are used to being catered to and having businesses compete for their attention. The danger of being a passive filter is that it encourages young adults to wait to be told what to buy, what to do, where to go, and what to believe, thereby losing their voice.

Technological advancements have greatly influenced the rise of U.S. consumerism and had a great impact on young adults. "Technology enabled [young adults] to have solidarity with other young adults around the world. . . . [It] was the key to forming a shared generational culture amid a world of tension and ambiguity."[41] Technology "gave access to what has been called a culture of simulation . . . (or imitation) of reality found in video culture—for example in film, music video and video games[.]"[42] Video has lulled young adults into thinking that they can be present to things even though they are physically absent, while it has made it possible to be present in this age of social distancing. "The accessibility of cheap recording devices made it possible to 'privatize' popular[/U.S.] culture."[43] And by privatizing the culture, faith was privatized.

Because Generation X is the first generation to be linked to popular culture, it is important to understand their relationship with the culture in order to better understand the Millennial generation's relationship. "Between Generation X and popular culture, then, there is a profound symbiosis. GenX cannot be understood apart from popular culture, and much of popular culture cannot be interpreted without attention to Generation X. . . . Pop culture provides the matrix that contains much of what counts as 'meaning' for [this] generation."[44] Since the Millennial generation is the first generation to come of age "digitally connected" from childhood, not adulthood, they too cannot be understood as separate from dominant U.S. popular culture.

Technology has made "information . . . far more accessible to the average person through mass media and most recently, the Internet. In addition, information has become more diverse. . . . Young adults at the start of the twenty-first century had easier access, not only to factual information but also to the arts, than any previous generation."[45] With so much information available, young adults have learned "that ideas and opinions are not written in stone. As opportunities to switch channels and surf Web sites proliferate, [young adults] also gain the ability to follow [their] whims."[46] In following their whims, young adults are less committed than previous generations. They are also more indecisive, knowing that something else will soon come along. "Electronic communications [,therefore,] represent the biggest cultural revolutions of recent times, with the arrival of radio, then television, and finally computers and information technology. The very rhythms of human consciousness have been altered by this world of fast-moving data and of images."[47]

This world of fast-moving data and images has led to globalization and technological advances that have opened many avenues for people, especially Millennial young adults. The opportunities to experience a variety of things from around the world; the fragility of creation (human, plant, and animal life); the freedom to believe anything; the disruption of family systems; the privatization of so many things have led to the need for young adults to connect with a community—the social aspect of humanity. For "it's harder to be in community now than it ever had been before because of the social isolation that we are experiencing and the greater effort it takes to move your way into community. Seldom is the community coming out to meet you. Most communities, particularly church communities, particularly Catholic church communities . . . presume the people will find their way in."[48] Millennials are not finding their way into the Church as much as we would like, therefore, Catholic church communities must be attentive to the ways young adults develop community in order to become communities attractive to young adults. One way that young adults have found community is in and through hip-hop.

HIP-HOP AND ITS INFLUENCE

In the United States, hip-hop is a cultural phenomenon that speaks loudly of the needs, concerns, desires, and dreams of young adults. Due to the popularity of hip-hop I was surprised to discover the roots of hip-hop in the African oral tradition. Raymond Codrington explains as follows:

> In the mid to late 1970s the cultural shockwave that would be known as hip hop emerged from the economic paralysis of New York City, especially the neglected black and Latino neighborhoods in the Bronx. However, while hip hop music was born in the Bronx, it both is part of and speaks to a long line of black American and African diasporic cultural traditions. Much of what is written about hip hop traces this culture through a series of stages, from a music- and dance-focused phenomenon created for and by people "on the block" to a dominant global youth culture. Many observers also make a connection between rap and West African *griot* tradition, the art of wandering storytellers known for their knowledge of local settings and superior vocal skills. Additionally, rhymed verses are an important part of African American culture in both the public and private realms.[49]

Codrington brings into focus the need for young people to speak out about the things happening around them and to them. Because the "hip-hop culture . . . is part of [an] extensive multiracial and cross-cultural field of social practice,"[50] it is able to speak to a generation in a way no other genre has.

> [B]arrio youth who produced hip-hop culture have unfolded a deeper understanding of difference and lofty notions of human community. The hip-hop culture that began with youth of color in post-industrial New York City has become a powerful source of youth [/young adult] identity and social criticism. . . . For the ever-evolving and complex constituency of this youth[/young adult] popular culture, hip-hop matters for young people who desire to articulate their theological and political sensibilities in the landscape of prophetic witness.[51]

Hip-hop allows youth/young adults to establish roots, define their purpose, define themselves, and create a collective identity.[52] It taps into young adults' need to speak and be heard. "It is hip hop that encourages kids to dream, tell their story of suffering, struggle, and pain."[53] In and through this genre, the spoken word, rap, is lifted to a place of honor—has a cultural currency—that speaks to young adults today because it is multiracial, multicultural, and multilinguistic.

> Although a great deal of ink has been used to explain rap music as an exclusively black American ethno-musical innovation, not only was it the product of black and Puerto Rican youths, but . . . it is best understood as the expression of the "cultural hybridity" of the postindustrial urban world. In other words, rap is not strictly speaking black music nor Puerto Rican music; rather, it is the sound of a multiracial, multicultural, and multilinguistic world.[54]

What is important is the "multiracial, multicultural, and multilinguistic world" young adults are maturing in. This understanding gives weight to a culture that speaks for a generation that is often said to be the most diverse generation of all time.

Ministers, church leadership, and catechists should take note of the influence of a profit-driven society on young adults, to which hip-hop speaks. With

> [y]outh in the United States growing up in a profit-driven society where millions of individuals who live in the shadow of prosperity experience life as a period between suffering and death . . . [y]outh who feel demoralized and powerless under the weight of our society's economic and political culture are . . . not entirely silenced. . . . Drawing on the resources of popular cultural forms such as hip-hop, a growing number of youth across various racial and ethnic communities find a message that says that the path toward constructing a more livable and humane world can be found[.][55]

Though not every Church ministry needs to embrace hip-hop, it is important to note well this phenomenon that affects the faith formation of young adults. "Hip hop claims to have God, to know God, to talk directly to God, to hear from God, and therefore, can bypass institutionalized religious authority."[56]

Hip-hop culture is not without its own problems. The danger of hip-hop is that young adults "without an understanding [of themselves,] are perpetually looking for media images to model [themselves] after; [they] are insatiable consumers of prepackaged 'cool.' "[57] Here again we see the role culture plays in shaping the identity of the consumer, particularly young adults. Though hip-hop has the ability to give voice to a generation seeking their voice, hip-hop has also fallen to U.S. consumerism and become a commodity to be bought and sold. "The urban form of expression that started in the ghettos of

New York City has emerged as a ten-billion-dollars-a-year industry."[58] As such, hip-hop becomes a powerful tool in shaping the behavior and world-view of young adults[59] in search of their true self.

IDENTITY

In and through story we not only find our identity, share our lives, but also form community, both secular and sacred. Young adults know this as evidenced by the growth in social network websites that promote community virtually. Young adults even search for God in this manner. Robert Wuthnow states that when it comes to the sacred,

> religious ideas among young adults probably circulate more by word of mouth than through the books and magazines people read or even the sermons they hear. This means that young adults are probably influencing one another in forming opinions about religion much more than they are being shaped by the formal teaching of religious organizations. We are in this sense a culture besieged with information, and yet a society in which so much information has forced us to improvise, to rely on our friends and our personal experiences, and to view all information from published sources with a healthy dose of skepticism.[60]

Young adults in their search for community are also learning to live into a new identity as an adult. They are asking, "Who am I? What am I going to contribute? Where do I fit?"[61] Determining where one fits is difficult, however, when the perceived foundation keeps changing. "[Young adults] coming of age in a society that has no unified or clear corporate identity would have a more challenging time coming to name their personal identity and integrate into adulthood, thus drawing out the passage through adolescence more than ever before."[62]

Young adults are not the only ones seeking to know who they are. "In the United States the African American has continually questioned his or her identity."[63] This continued quest to understand identity follows a progression, and is a journey. Storytelling is the vehicle that records the process. Young adults, often marginalized like Blacks in America, need this expressive way to tell their story and hear another's. African-American storytelling draws on this situation and gives young adults a place in which to ground themselves while they examine their story using the Christian Story.

The examination of the Christian Story requires a look into history, the subject of least interest to many young adults:

> In a recent survey, new college graduates listed history as the academic subject whose lessons they found of least use in their daily affairs. In part, this reflects

the show-me pragmatism of today's rising generation. . . . Many [people] have difficulty placing their own thoughts and actions, even their own lives, in any larger story. . . . If history seems of little personal relevance today, then what we do today seems of equal irrelevance to our own lives (and the lives of others) tomorrow. Without a sense of trajectory, the future becomes almost random. So why not live for today? What's to lose?[64]

The search for purpose and identity is directly related to the lack of story. If *My Story-Your Story* is not told, it is not heard; if it is not heard, there is no history. As Strauss and Howe stated above, when history is no longer important, where you are going, and your journey and destination are confusing. African-American storytelling will help young adults reclaim their identity by looking into their own story and finding their place in the larger story. As Vincent Miller argues:

[The] use of narrative to sell merchandise gives rise to the most profound cultural impact of . . . producers of commercial popular culture: the formation of our habits of interpretation and appropriation. As children, young adults learn[ed] to quickly accept narratives, to enjoy the roles and symbol systems of the stories, to locate themselves within the tales. . . . While [they were] learning to do all this, they were simultaneously learning to treat these narratives, roles, and symbols as disposable commodities: things to be played with, explored, tried on, and, in the end, discarded.[65]

African-American storytelling reintroduces narrative to young adults by helping them not only find their place in the story but also understand the importance of their story to the Story.[66] Instead of discarding the story when they think they are finished with it, African-American storytelling allows them to grow in and through their story for the Story.

SPIRITUALITY/SPIRITUAL AWARENESS

Robert Wuthnow likens the religion and spirituality of young adults to "a cultural bricolage,"[67] or tinkering. He states, "tinkers are the most resourceful people in any era. If specialized skills are required, they have them. When they need help from experts, they seek it. But they do not rely on only one way of doing things. Their approach to life is practical. They get things done, and usually this happens by improvising, by piecing together an idea from here, a skill from there, and a contact from somewhere else."[68] This is the "religious landscape" of many Millennial young adults because "our world is filled with the kinds of uncertainty that make tinkering a necessity."[69]

For young adults, this tinkering is not limited to work, socializing, family, or friends. This tinkering also includes religion and faith.

> [Young adults] piece together [their] thoughts about religion and interests in spirituality from the materials at hand. . . . The possibilities of tinkering increase with the expansion of available information and exposure to diverse cultures and networks. . . . The spiritual tinkerer is able to sift through a veritable scrap heap of ideas and practices from childhood, from religious organizations, classes, conversations with friends, books, magazines, television programs, and Web sites. . . . Especially in young adulthood, the institutional restraints that might prevent it are absent.[70]

With restraints missing, young adults are searching for God in the things they experience and encounter. "Young people are growing up in a society that considers finding God in the details of popular culture important; indeed, the messages they receive is that a way to remain open to the sacred is to pay attention to the complex variety of religious possibilities available in human experience."[71] In this openness, the Story often gets lost because it has been devalued, in search of something else. "Fr. Clarence Rivers . . . points out that biblical peoples, along with Black peoples, are primarily from oral-aural traditions. Such peoples value the poetic over and above the conceptual and personal involvement over analytical detachment."[72] Given the technological explosion of video and spoken word as evidenced in video games, cellular phones, videoconferencing, and video-chat that young adults experience, I conclude that young adults, like Black people, are an oral-aural people. This understanding of young adults is important to accompanying them as they seek to find God in a fashion often different from our own. Young adults are the inheritors of an era that has "altered the cultural conditions of possibility of the 'hearing' from which Christian faith is born[.]"[73]

This chapter has traced generational shifts and described key elements of the culture and context of young adults today. I offered particular attention to technology and to hip-hop as well as the role of narrative in young adults' lives today—each exerts force on the shaping of their identity and spirituality today. This look at young adults opens the door to African-American storytelling and intergenerational catechesis by identifying connection points for interaction. These connection points are at the root of *My Story-Your Story*.

Given the oral-aural quality of young adults' experience, I posit in the next chapter that African-American storytelling has the potential to return the oral-aural nature of the gospel to our lives as we live into social distancing via video-chat and videoconferencing. By returning to the gospel's oral-aural nature, African-American storytelling not only lifts the voices of young adults, but it also lifts the voices of other generations by making room for one another.[74] Thus, storytelling makes it possible for catechists to better reecho the Catholic faith.

NOTES

1. timone newsome, "Millennial Young Adults: Shapeshifters," *Church* (Fall 2008, Center Section): 13–15.

2. timone davis, "Cultural Colonization and Young Adult Liturgical Experience," *The Journal of the Black Catholic Theological Symposium* 12 (2019): 87–104.

3. The Five Generations of Computers, Google, accessed February 29, 2020, "The history of computer development is often referred to in reference to the different generations of computing devices. Each generation of computer is characterized by a major technological development that fundamentally changed the way computers operate, resulting in increasingly smaller, cheaper, more powerful and more efficient and reliable devices," https://www.sites.google.com/site/btcsit/generations-of-comp uters, accessed February 29, 2020. Also see *Webster's Unabridged Dictionary of the English Language* (Random House, Inc., 2001).

4. Robert Wuthnow, *After the Baby Boomers: How Twenty- and Thirty-Somethings Are Shaping the Future of American Religion* (Princeton University Press, 2010), 3.

5. *Webster's Unabridged Dictionary of the English Language* (Random House, Inc., 2001).

6. Paul Taylor and Scott Keeter, eds. "Millennials: A Portrait of Generation Next: Confident. Connected. Open to Change," *Pew Research Center*, February 21, 2010, from the preface, accessed March 2, 2020, www.pewresearch.org/millennials. This publication is part of a Pew Research Center report series that looks at the values, attitudes, and experiences of America's next generation: The Millennials.

7. Hayim Herring, *Connecting Generations: Bridging the Boomer, Gen X, and Millennial Divide* (Lanham, MD: Rowman & Littlefield, 2019), viii.

8. Michael Paul Gallagher, *Clashing Symbols: An Introduction to Faith and Culture* (New York/Mahwah, NJ: Paulist Press, 2003), 99.

9. Gallagher, 110.

10. Gallagher, 7.

11. "Generational Birth Years," *The Center for Generational Kinetics*, accessed February 29, 2020, https://genhq.com/generational_birth_years/. "It's really important to note that you can be born within three years on either side of the beginning or ending of a generation and have all the characteristics of the generation before or after. This has to do with a number of factors including the age of your parents, if you grew up in an urban or rural environment, affluence, education and more. Being raised in a military household can also change your generational identity."

12. "Generational Differences Chart," *StudyLib*, accessed February 29, 2020, https://studylib.net/doc/8718132/generational-differences-chart. Dennis Gaylor,

"Generational Differences," *U.S. Fish and Wild Life*, accessed May 6, 2020, https://tr aining.fws.gov/supervisors/update/episode2/documents/generationaldifferenceschar t.pdf.

13. William D'Antonio, James D. Davidson, Dean R. Hoge, and Mary L Gautier, *American Catholics Today: New Realities of Their Faith and Their Church* (Lanham: Rowman and Littlefield Publishers, Inc., 2007), 18.

14. Dean R. Hoge, William D. Dinges, Mary Johnson, and Juan L. Gonzales, Jr., *Young Adult Catholics: Religion in the Culture of Choice* (Notre Dame, IN: University of Notre Dame Press, 2001), 11.

15. *Merriam-Webster*, accessed March 4, 2020, http://www.merriam-webster.com /dictionary/latchkey+child?show=0&t=1300736489.

16. Tom Beaudoin, *Virtual Faith: The Irreverent Spiritual Quest of Generation X* (San Francisco: Jossey-Bass, 1998), 5.

17. *Merriam-Webster*, accessed March 4, 2020, http://www.merriam-webster.com /dictionary/middle%20class.

18. Paul VI, "The Apostolic Exhortation on Evangelization in the Modern World *Evangelii Nunutiandi* (1975)," in *The Catechetical Documents: A Parish Resource* (Chicago: Liturgy Training Publications, 1996), 27. Subsequent references will be made parenthetically citing *EN*. "Evangelization will also always contain—as the foundation, center and at the same time summit of its dynamism—a clear proclama- tion that, in Jesus Christ, the Son of God made man, who died and rose from the dead, salvation is offered to all men, as a gift of God's grace and mercy."

19. D'Antonio, Davidson, Hoge, and Gautier, 19.

20. Harold J. Recinos, "Transforming Ecclesiology: Hip-Hop Matters," in *In Our Own Voices: Latino/a Renditions of Theology*, ed. Benjamin Valentin (Maryknoll, NY: Orbis Books, 2010), 156.

21. "'Nones' on the Rise," *Pew Research Center*, October 9, 2012, accessed February 29, 2020, https://www.pewforum.org/2012/10/09/nones-on-the-rise/.

22. Michael Dimock, "Defining Generations: Where Millennials End and Generation Z Begins," *Pew Research Center*, January 17, 2019, accessed February 29, 2020.www.pewresearch.org/fact-tank/2019/01/17/where-millennials-end-and -generation-z-begins/.

23. Dimcock, "Defining Generations."

24. Stephen B. Bevans, *Models of Contextual Theology: Faith and Cultures*, rev. ed. (Maryknoll, NY: Orbis Books, 2002), 4.

25. Bevans, 6.

26. John Fonte, "E Pluribus Unum: The Bradley Project on America's National Identity," *The Bradley Project*, June 1, 2008, accessed March 14, 2020. https://ww w.hudson.org/research/14149-e-pluribus-unum-the-bradley-project-on-america-s-nat ional-identity.

27. Fonte, 4–5.

28. Beaudoin, xiv.

29. Taylor and Keeter, 25.

30. Theresa O'Keefe, "Mentoring Relationships in Ministry to Youth and Young Adults," Boston College, The Church in the 21st Century Center, recorded October

29, 2009, accessed March 4, 2020, https://www.youtube.com/watch?v=Z0HdV-jS prU&t=74s.

31. Juliet B. Schor, *Born to Buy: The Commercialized Child and the New Consumer Culture* (New York: Scribner, 2004), 13.

32. Schor, 16.

33. Theresa O' Keefe, "The Same But Different: The Culture in Which Our Adolescents Live," *Journal of Youth and Theology* 7, no. 2 (November 2008): 49.

34. Schor, 9.

35. Vincent J. Miller, *Consuming Religion: Christian Faith and Practice in a Consumer Culture* (New York: Continuum, 2005), 179.

36. Miller, 225.

37. Wuthnow, 49.

38. Taylor and Keeter, 1.

39. Mike Hayes, *Googling God: The Religious Landscape of People in their 20s and 30s* (New York/Mahwah, NJ: Paulist Press, 2007), xii.

40. Christian Piatt and Amy Piatt, *MySpace to Sacred Space: God for a New Generation* (St. Louis: Chalice Press, 2007), 15.

41. Beaudoin, 11.

42. Beaudoin, 13.

43. Beaudoin, 5–6.

44. Beaudoin, 22.

45. Wuthnow, 45.

46. Wuthnow, 47.

47. Gallagher, 79–80.

48. O'Keefe, "Mentoring Relationships in Ministry to Youth and Young Adults."

49. Raymond Codrington, "In the Beginning: Hip-hop's Early Influences," *Oxford African American Studies Center*, accessed March 2, 2020, http://www.oxfordaasc .com/public/features/archive/0806/essay.jsp.

50. Recinos, 161.

51. Recinos, 157.

52. Raquel Z. Rivera, *New York Ricans from the Hip-hop Zone* (New York: Palgrave Macmillan, 2003), xii.

53. Ralph C. Watkins, "From Black Theology and Black Power to Afrocentric Theology and Hip Hop Power: And Extension and Socio-Re-Theological Conceptualization of Cone's Theology in Conversation with the Hip Hop Generation," *Black Theology: An International Journal* 8, no. 3 (2010): 334.

54. Recinos, 168–169.

55. Recinos, 158–159.

56. Watkins, 332.

57. Rivera, xii.

58. Tommy Kyllonen, *Un.orthodox: Church, Hip-Hop, Culture* (Grand Rapids, MI: Zondervan, 2007), 99.

59. Kyllonen, 88.

60. Wuthnow, 120.

61. O'Keefe, "Mentoring Relationships in Ministry to Youth and Young Adults."

62. O'Keefe, "The Same But Different," 43–44.

63. Linda Goss and Marian E. Barnes, eds. *Talk that Talk: An Anthology of African-American Storytelling* (New York: Simon and Schuster, 1989), 13.

64. William Strauss and Neil Howe, *Generations: The History of America's Future, 1584 to 2069* (New York: William Morrow, 1991), 7.

65. Miller, 5–6.

66. The capitalization of story is to denote the Christian Story from Salvation History through the Crucifixion and Resurrection of Jesus.

67. Wuthnow, xvii.

68. Wuthnow, 13–14.

69. Wuthnow, 14.

70. Wuthnow, 15.

71. Recinos, 157.

72. Nathan Jones, *Sharing the Old, Old Story: Educational Ministry in the Black Community* (Winona, MN: St. Mary's Press, 1982), 45.

73. Gallagher, 80.

74. Pope Francis, *Christ is Alive! Christus Vivit: Post-synodal Apostolic Exhortation* (Washington, DC: United States Conference of Catholic Bishops, 2019), 38. Subsequent references will be made parenthetically citing *CV*.

Chapter 2

Storytelling

Ancient and New

Then beginning with Moses and all the prophets, he interpreted to them the things about himself in all the scriptures.

—Luke 24:27

I love a good story, one that draws me in and invites me to participate. Our living is filled with story. It's the way we share what is happening to us and around us. Story stretches us—asks that we lean toward the storyteller. The storyteller, the person with the situation, weaves a tale—a story, while the listener takes it all in and situates him-/herself around the story being told. Our stories connect our lives. Through that connection, we find that "storytelling is a fundamental way of codifying hard-won truths and dramatizing the rationale behind traditions. Thus, the tales will often end with 'a message,' a point, a truth to remember as one confronts life's problems."[1] In various settings and circumstances, we find people relating to events through story. Families recount stories of ancestors and traditions, while creating new stories at each gathering. Businesses use story to draw people to their product or service. A company's "About Us" tab on their website is sure to get quite a few clicks from people looking into not only what they offer but who they are. The Church, rooted in the Salvation History of Christians, asks us to become participants in that Story today. "Story is a means whereby people come to terms with their lives, their past; it is a way of understanding their relationship within the context of their traditions. It is a means of accessing and valuing history: in the end, story is history."[2]

Storytelling is so much a part of our lives that we often don't recognize it. "Like all human activity, [it] is situated, its form, meaning, and functions rooted in culturally defined scenes or events—bounded segments of the flow of behavior and experience that constitute meaningful contexts for action, interpretation, and evaluation."[3] This phenomenon of telling a story to share our ideas, situations, and circumstances presents the Catholic Church with a way to catechize those seeking ways to connect with the Church; those who attend church regularly; those who are seeking a deeper understanding of faith and those who aren't sure what they are seeking. "Storytelling is a universal experience shared by every social group";[4] however, it is important to recognize that "the structure and process of storying—how stories are told, by whom, to whom, under what circumstances, and for what specific purpose—vary according to sociocultural prescriptions."[5] It is precisely because of its universal nature that storytelling can be used as a method of catechesis for revitalizing people of faith.

I didn't always think of story as part of everyday living. I used to think story was only in the books I was reading: historical romance, mysteries, and thrillers. Then, I started paying closer attention to what Jesus is asking us to do in Matthew 28:19, "Go therefore and make disciples of all nations, baptizing them in the name of the Father and of the Son and of the Holy Spirit, and teaching them to obey everything that I have commanded you." This call to baptize and teach is anchored in the story. We tell the story of Jesus to awaken for others, the love of God for them, and to deepen our understanding of God's love for us. With this expanded understanding of story, I began to look at what made African-American storytelling unique. I discovered that African-American storytelling has its roots in the African oral tradition.

In this chapter, I explore the African oral tradition as it is revealed in African folktales. I show how African folktales evolved into African-American tales with a discussion on why these tales were important to the survival of the people. I then take a look at the relationship between African-American storytelling, faith, scripture, and preaching, before ending with freedom through story.

AFRICAN ORIGINS OF STORYTELLING

Rooted in the African oral tradition, African-American storytelling as a method of catechesis has the potential to revitalize people's faith. Roger Abrahams in *African Folktales* supports this when he talks about how the strength of story can unite people in ways the written word cannot, creating bridges rather than chasms.[6] Why is story so important, so powerful? According to Anne Shimojima, there are twelve reasons to value story.[7] Story, she states:

- enhances imagination and visualization
- develops appreciation of the beauty and rhythm of language

- increases vocabulary
- refines speaking skills
- improves listening skills
- allows [multiple generations] to interact on a personal level
- enhances writing skills
- develops reading skills and sparks interest in reading
- enhances critical and creative thinking skills
- nourishes [people's] intuitive side
- helps [people] see literature as a mirror of human experiences
- helps [people] understand their own and others' cultural heritage

Shimojima's list of values depicts how story transforms not only the storyteller's life but also the lives of the listeners.

The African oral tradition, rooted in griots (pronounced GREE-ohs)— caretakers of the collective story, helps us understand how stories share the history, the customs, and values of people.[8] "Such traditional pieces of knowledge are passed primarily by observation, common experience, and explicit word-of-mouth transmission."[9] This commitment to storytelling did not stop even as Africans found themselves in chains and shipped around the world. Story encouraged enslaved Africans to maintain aspects of the past for use in their present circumstance. "Ironically, the dehumanizing conditions of slavery, its prohibitions against literacy, against African language and ritual, reinforced the communal values of the oral tradition."[10]

In order to reinforce values, story has to invite dialogue that results in action. That was the role of the African oral tradition. Linking Shimojima's list of values with the African oral tradition, we discover that storytelling provides the listener with information that calls him/her into action. Catechesis that uses story rooted in the African oral tradition calls people forward to grow in faith through a personal relationship with Jesus lived out in and through relationships with others. "A catalytic process, African oral storytelling expresses the flux of social and natural reality through its open form."[11]

THE EVOLUTION OF AFRICAN-AMERICAN STORYTELLING

The African oral tradition of folktales as told by the griot emerged as something new as African-American storytellers added their experiences in the United States to the stories brought by African slaves:

Despite the severe restrictions against the preservation of indigenous African cultural forms, and the concomitant legal prohibitions against literacy mastery, black people merged what they could retain from their African heritage with forms that they could appropriate from the various New World cultures into which they had been flung. The blends that they forged . . . was a new culture. . . . In the instance of the African in America, a truly African-American expressive culture emerged from deep inside the bowels of enslavement. This African-American culture was a veritable "underground" culture, shared . . . by word of mouth.[12]

This underground culture was expressed in the stories of my childhood when my mother would remind me there are certain "ways of being" in the United States for an African-American female. It is also being expressed today, as we witness video footage of Black people being harassed, beaten, imprisoned, and killed for being Black.

African-Americans use stories to help them learn how they "should and should not act to be useful members of society, community, and family."[13] These stories are now being told via social media. In the Catholic Church, we too use stories to help us learn about creation and our God, who we are and our origins as people, and what we are to do. "The challenge right now is that we are immersed in vast oceans of stories, and increasingly our efforts to make sense of them cluster around the dynamics of authenticity and agency."[14] No matter our age, we can find ourselves asking, "Who am I? What am I called to do?" Henry Louis Gates Jr. explains how stories become the foundation of beliefs and values:

Telling ourselves our own stories—interpreting the nature of our world to ourselves, asking and answering epistemological and ontological questions in our own voices and on our own terms—has as much as any single factor been responsible for the survival of African-Americans and their culture. The stories that we tell ourselves and our children function to order our world, serving to create both a foundation upon which each of us constructs our sense of reality and a filter through which we process each event that confronts us every day. The values that we cherish and wish to preserve, the behavior that we wish to censure, the fear and dread that we can barely confess in ordinary language, the aspirations and goals that we most dearly prize—all of these things are encoded in the stories that each culture invents and preserves for the next generation, stories that, in effect, we live by and through. And the stories that survive, the stories that manage to resurface under different guises and with marvelous variations, these are a culture's canonical tales, the tales that contain the cultural codes that are assumed or internalized by members of that culture. For the African American, deprived by law of the tools of literacy, the narration of these stories in black vernacular forms served to bring together the several colorful fragments of lost African cultures in a spectacularly blended weave that we call African American culture.[15]

This strategy was important particularly among Blacks who needed to convey information undetected not only to children but to other Blacks, slaves, and/or free. "African-Americans nurtured a private but collective oral culture, one they could not 'write down,' but one they created, crafted, shared with each other and preserved for subsequent generations out loud, but outside of the hearing of the white people who enslaved them, and, later, discriminated against them."[16] This method of teaching continued to be important after the emancipation of slaves so that Blacks could protect themselves through times just as serious as slavery, that is, Jim Crow segregation. "The cultural and social practices of West Africa traveled with Africans as they crossed the waters to the United States. Despite the horrors of slavery, Africans [now in diaspora] still told stories to comfort, teach, and record history in their new home. . . . These storytelling traditions continued from slavery through Jim Crowism, to the Civil Rights movement, and on to present day America."[17]

AFRICAN-AMERICAN STORYTELLING, FAITH, AND SCRIPTURE

African slaves were able to keep alive their culture in a strange land while enduring oppressive conditions by telling the stories of their homeland. As slavery continued and the African tales became the tales of African-Americans, both free and slaves, transformations were recorded. One well-noted arena of holding on to one's culture and transforming it into something new was in religion.

> In the New World slave control was based on the eradication of all forms of African culture because of their power to unify the slaves and thus enable them to resist or rebel. Nevertheless, African beliefs and customs persisted and were transmitted by the slaves to their descendants. . . . African styles of worship, forms of ritual, systems of belief, and fundamental perspectives have remained vital on this side of the Atlantic, not because they were preserved in a "pure" orthodoxy but because they were transformed.[18]

By listening to the stories of the Bible, the African slaves and their descendants discovered the God who rescues—who "makes a way out of no way."

The Story of God at work in the lives of the people God loves is told again and again in order to gain new truths. As enslaved African-Americans continued listening to the stories of the Bible, "one story in particular caught their attention and fascinated them with its implications and potential applications to their own situation. That story was the story of Exodus."[19]

By appropriating the story of Exodus as their own story, black Christians articulated their own sense of peoplehood. . . . Exodus became dramatically real, especially in the song and prayer meetings of the slaves who reenacted the story as they shuffle in the ring dance they called the "Shout."[20]

This integration of the biblical story into their daily living is precisely the gift of African-American storytelling. As a method of catechesis, it allows everyone to integrate scripture and Catholic traditions into their lives whereby they will be transformed. For the enslaved African and African-American, telling the story of Exodus allowed "an ancient, historic event [to] remain an ever-present reality to a faithful people. The retelling of the Story [was] not merely a recollection of the past, but a drawing of the past events into the present."[21] As we continue to search for understanding we will need African-American storytelling to help us form community and gain hope in growing in faith. "African American forebears in slavery were cognizant of the Bible as a storied document with which they could link their own stories, and from which they could find direction and hope in the hard trials and tribulations of their circumstances. Their storytelling continued a revered African ancestral manner of relating in community. It allowed them to reveal the depth of their own experiences and pose tough questions about life."[22] Nathan Jones reminds us, "Each one of us has a story to tell. God is continually unfolding his revelation in our personal and collective lives. This process of reflection/action/reflection is aimed at identifying our story in God's Story and God's Story in ours."[23] Once we identify this, we are better able to see how biblical stories provide truth to us each time they are read at different times in our lives.

AFRICAN-AMERICAN STORYTELLING
AND PREACHING

In the Catholic Church today there is a battle cry that often rises above the noise of many complaints: We need relevant preaching! I too have voiced that cry after sitting through yet another sermon that seems so far away from my daily living. African-American storytelling can help make preaching not only relevant but also engaging. In order to do this well, the preacher must first write a sermon that is grounded in scripture and the life of the people. "The sermon is more than exegesis, translations, word studies, and academic research on a text or topic. It cannot be divorced from the being, experience, imagination and dreams of the preacher nor the imagination and dreams of the preacher. To be a sermon, it cannot be an essay or poem apart from the complex life experiences of the preacher."[24] It is the preacher's responsibility to take the intimate knowledge gained through experience and share it in the sermon so that others may come to know God working in and through their living. Preaching, as a form of storytelling, must have facts that the preacher has personally experienced and/or the preacher must be able to tell a story that appeals to the imagination, calling up experience. The sermon then is a story of people connecting their lives to God. "The Black preacher has historically been adept in fostering and creating a new, more livable world in the minds of his or her hearers by appealing to the imagination as an interpretive tool. . . . The sanctified imagination of Black preachers is akin to the discourse of novels and poetry, where the writer imagines another world and takes the reader there."[25] Like African-American tales, the sermon may use fictional characters to ensure the message of the gospel is understood. "This world of the gospel is not 'real,' not available until this credible utterance, [the sermon], authorizes a departure from [the] text. . . . This imagined world allows one to cope with the evils and injustices in the world."[26]

Since it is important that the preacher ground the sermon in experience, it stands that the people, the congregation, are quite important. So important is the congregation that "black preaching creates a dialogue with the hearers. . . . This worship style reflects the larger dialogical, West African oral culture. Black congregations feel free to express themselves, which is seen as meaningful participation in the preaching event."[27] The shouting of "Amen" and "preach preacher" from members in the congregation are examples of people getting involved in the sermon as if it was a story being told in a different setting. "Such participation can help people to remember what they celebrate and put those experiences to work in their daily lives."[28] When I hear the preacher say something that resonates in my life, my shouting "Amen" or "Yes" is the verbal acknowledgment that I am either doing the right thing or need to start doing the right thing. It is my way of saying, "Yes Lord, I hear You." "Call-and-response is both a fundamental, perhaps even universal oral mode and a distinctively African and African-American form of discourse in speech and story, sermons and songs. . . . As it evolves in the black American oral tradition, the call-and-response pattern registers the changing relationship between the individual . . . [the] storyteller and the community."[29]

The dialogical nature of preaching using African-American storytelling will engage everyone in a way that allows them to take words spoken and apply them to their personal lives. Preaching that comes through experience— my story, touches experience—your story, creating a connection that calls for change. Faith formation assists us in changing—transforming ourselves into imitators of Jesus.

FREEDOM THROUGH STORY: THE LIBERATING
EFFECTS OF AFRICAN-AMERICAN STORYTELLING

African-American storytelling aptly expresses freedom because "African American culture, first and foremost, is a resistance culture dynamically constructed around the thematic ideas of freedom and justice. . . . The African American community has always understood that those whom the Spirit makes free are free indeed."[30] This reference to spiritual freedom is reflected in the stories African-Americans tell to help people understand their situation. The stories are not only for others but for African-Americans themselves. African-American storytelling lights a path for those who wish to combat the current cultural tendency of individualism and exclusion by becoming a "resistant" culture, "refusing to be dominated by an opposing value system."[31]

These different experiences allow African-American storytelling to be a method that gives voice to each generation's spiritual self. "The spiritual journey requires that we attend to our voices and to the possibilities that they contain. We cannot walk on the journey of faith if we do not notice our voices and what they reveal to us about ourselves."[32] Since stories provide self-revelation in addition to creating a foundation, it is important that we see story as freeing:

> [L]iberation is often expressed and experienced through testimonies and stories. . . . [African-Americans] have a strong heritage of invoking the voices of the ancestors and past experiences through storytelling. The sharing of the narratives provides a living legacy of history, morality, ethics, theology, and spirituality. [African-Americans] experienced the liberating power of God through the living testimonies and stories they shared with one another.[33]

African-American storytelling opens each generation more fully to who they themselves are and who "other" is. In doing so, their voices are freed in a way that both liberates them and challenges them to press forward in faith in God. "The freed voice is the voice involved in the search for self and other, but that is self-defining."[34] Catechesis that uses African-American storytelling affords each generation the ability to learn and name their faith setting each person free in faith.

NOTES

1. Roger D. Abrahams, *African Folktales: Traditional Stories of the Black World* (New York: Pantheon Books, 1983), xvi.
2. Harold Scheub, *Story* (Madison: The University of Wisconsin Press, 1998), 21.

3. Richard Bauman, *Story, Performance and Event* (Cambridge University Press, 1986), 3.

4. Jan Carter-Black, "Teaching Cultural Competence: An Innovative Strategy Grounded in the Universality of Storytelling as Depicted in African and African American Storytelling Traditions," *Journal of Social Work Education* 43, no. 1 (2007): 32.

5. Carter-Black, 32.

6. Abrahams, *African Folktales*, 1–2.

7. Anne Shimojima, "This Is Why I Tell It: The Value of Telling Stories," in *The Power of Story: Teaching through Storytelling*, eds. Rives Collins and Pamela Cooper (Long Grove, IL: Waveland Press, Inc., 2005), 11–18.

8. Nathan Jones, *Sharing the Old, Old Story: Educational Ministry in the Black Community* (Winona, MN: St. Mary's Press, 1982), 72.

9. Abrahams, *African Folktales*, 20.

10. John F. Callahan, *In the African-American Grain: Call and Response in Twentieth-Century Black Fiction* (University of Illinois Press, 2001), 26.

11. Callahan, 15.

12. Henry Louis Gates, Jr., "Introduction: Narration and Cultural Memory in the African-American Tradition," in *Talk That Talk: An Anthology of African-American Storytelling*, eds. Linda Goss and Marian E. Barnes (New York: Simon and Schuster, 1989), 16–17.

13. Abrahams, *African Folktales*, 23–24.

14. Mary E. Hess, "Finding a Way into Empathy through Story Exercises in a Religious Studies Classroom," *Religious Studies News*, accessed October 19, 2020, https://rsn.aarweb.org/spotlight-on/teaching/empathy/story-exercises-religious-studies-classroom.

15. Gates, Jr., 17–18.

16. Gates, Jr., 17.

17. Tempii B. Champion, *Understanding Storytelling Among African American Children: A Journey From Africa to America* (Mahwah, NJ: Lawrence Erlbaum Associates, Publishers, 2003), 3.

18. Albert J. Raboteau, *Slave Religion: The "Invisible Institution" in the Antebellum South*, 2nd ed. (Oxford University Press, 2004), 4.

19. Albert J. Raboteau, *A Fire in the Bones: Reflections on African-American Religious History* (Boston: Beacon Press, 1995), 18.

20. Raboteau, *A Fire in the Bones*, 33.

21. Jones, 8.

22. Anne E. Streaty Wimberly, *Soul Stories: African American Christian Education* (Nashville: Abingdon Press, 2005), 4. On this same page Wimberly expounds on storytelling when she states, "The ongoing call for story and storytelling in Christian education is, thus, a plea for us to recover the central role of story and storytelling for the liberating wisdom and hope-building vocation." Wimberly's approach to storytelling is entitled "story-linking." In this process she expounds upon the importance of using story to connect one's life to that of scripture in order to live out one's vocation.

23. Jones, 83.

24. James Henry Harris, *The Word Made Plain: The Power and Promise of Preaching* (Minneapolis: Fortress Press, 2004), 100–101.

25. Harris, 107.

26. Harris, 108.

27. Dale P. Andrews, *Practical Theology for Black Churches: Bridging Black Theology and African American Folk Religion* (Louisville: Westminster John Knox Press, 2002), 22.

28. Andrews, 23.

29. Callahan, 16–17.

30. Lee H. Butler, *Liberating Our Dignity, Saving Our Souls* (St. Louis: Chalice Press, 2006), 8–9.

31. Butler, 100.

32. Kenneth H. Hill, *Religious Education in the African American Tradition: A Comprehensive Introduction* (St. Louis: Chalice Press, 2007), 55.

33. Butler, 122.

34. Gayl Jones, *Liberating Voices: Oral Tradition in African American Literature* (Harvard University Press, 1991), 178.

Chapter 3

Story: Faith Formation and Catechesis

Give ear, O my people, to my teaching; incline your ears to the words of my mouth. I will open my mouth in a parable; I will utter dark sayings from of old, things that we have heard and known, that our ancestors have told us.

— *Psalm 78:1–3*

SCOPE AND THEOLOGY OF CATECHESIS

A person's knowledge is often determined through measurable means, by which assessments are designed and administered to calculate the level of knowing. When people reach certain standard markers, it can be said that they are knowledgeable to that degree. In order to reach these standards, people are educated in various subject areas: reading, writing, arithmetic, science, fine arts, to name a few. Knowledge of one's faith tradition doesn't escape this process. Though religious education, "that dimension of the church's ministry that seeks to bring the life story, cultural story, and Christian story into conversation, one with another,"[1] does not measure levels of faith, knowing is important. "The nature, purpose, and context of Christian religious education calls for a way of knowing that can hold past, present, and future in a fruitful tension, that fosters free and freeing lived Christian faith, that promotes a creative relationship with a Christian community and of that community with the world."[2] Holding the past in tension with the present in tension with the future requires teaching that reminds us of our connection to events, particularly events that shaped and shape faith traditions. Catechesis is that type of teaching. Catechesis "comes from the Greek verb *katéchein*, which means "to resound," "to echo," or "to hand down."[3] It "prepares the Christian to live in community and participate actively in the life and mission of the Church" (*GDC* 86). The notion of knowing then is less about achieving a standard, and more about being present as a person of faith. "All catechesis should have as its end goal the equipping of people with knowledge and tools that allow them to continue the building up of the Kingdom of God" (*GDC* 163).

The Reign of God first requires knowledge of God and that knowledge comes through stories of faith.[4] In handing down stories of faith, catechesis narrates the story of kin-dom as Christ-centered and community-centered. "Catechesis retells and relates the Story of God [and] the Story of the Catholic faith. . . . [It] is a ministry of God's Word and our words to one another."[5] By focusing on God's word and proclaiming it through the lens of lived experience, African-American storytelling as a method of catechesis "is incarnational in its theology, collegial in its style of leadership, creatively inclusive in its worship, and profoundly hopeful in its efforts toward greater conversion and justice in the world."[6] Through the use of African-American storytelling, people's concerns are addressed more candidly.

Addressing people's needs through *My Story-Your Story* puts both the "teacher" and "student" on even ground where they both realize the importance of each other. This relationship then illustrates how catechesis is more than transmitting knowledge, but is integral in strengthening faith through the word. "Catechesis aims therefore at developing understanding of the mystery of Christ in the light of God's word, so that the whole of a person's humanity is impregnated by that word."[7] Impregnating people with the word of God requires a relationship that goes beyond informational sharing toward sharing that calls us all to delve the depths of our own story and tell it. *My Story-Your Story* is "catechesis [that builds] on life and on the day-to-day experiences of real people. Our catechesis must endeavor to uncover the Good News in daily living: Where are God's messages in the raw details and dailiness of our lives?"[8]

Answering the question above involves our talking about God in our lives in and through the person of Jesus Christ. Pope John Paul II explains it this way:

[A]t the heart of catechesis we find, in essence, a Person, the Person of Jesus of Nazareth, . . . and Christian living consists in following Christ. . . . The primary and essential object of catechesis is . . . to reveal in the Person of Christ the whole of God's eternal design reaching fulfillment in that Person. It is to seek to understand the meaning of Christ's actions and words and of the signs worked by Him, for they simultaneously hide and reveal His mystery. Accordingly, the definitive aim of catechesis is to put people not only in touch but in communion, in intimacy, with Jesus Christ: only He can lead us to the love of the Father in the Spirit and make us share in the life of the Holy Trinity. (*CT* 5)

African-American storytelling provides us with a tool that allows for the intimacy called forth by John Paul II that is necessary to build personal relationships that then allows Jesus the person to enter in. With Jesus at the heart of catechesis we better understand why storytelling is important both in sharing the stories of Jesus and in sharing our individual stories. Storytelling builds the relationship.

Relationship built through the catechetical method of African-American storytelling "means that 'catechesis' must often concern itself not only with nourishing and teaching the faith, but also with arousing it unceasingly with the help of grace, with opening the heart, with converting, and with preparing total adherence to Jesus Christ on the part of those who are still on the threshold of faith. This concern will in part decide the tone, the language and the method of catechesis" (*CT* 19).

CATECHESIS AND EVANGELIZATION

Catechesis and evangelization are two sides of the same coin. Where catechesis tells again the stories of faith-filled people, evangelization tells the story of Jesus. Story, therefore, unites catechesis and evangelization. In telling my story or listening to your story the hope and love of God acting in our lives comes to life for our growth, our use. "Evangelization presupposes the witness of a life filled with hope and love."[9] This witness of life is in my story of faith. As I share my story of faith, it is my hope that it connects to your story and invites you to know more about the God of whom I speak. This is evangelization: "bringing the Good News into all the strata of humanity, and through its influence transforming humanity from within and making it new" (*EN* 18). Where catechesis reechoes stories of faith, evangelization is a living result of story. The gospel as story is told from different perspectives in scripture, to bring people to Christ. Those who come do so as a result of story. Evangelization therefore is a storytelling endeavor. "To evangelize others, the Christian community must constantly be evangelized, for the Gospel message needs to be heard anew in the many circumstances of life."[10] This "hearing again" occurs when we tell and listen to story. The African-American storytelling tradition gives us a process in which to keep the good news alive and relevant for our Christian living. "Shared experience, story telling, celebration, action, and reflection . . . within a community of faith best helps us understand how faith is transmitted, expanded, and sustained."[11]

As the story of Jesus evangelizes a person to "the Good News of the king-dom of God" (*EN* 14), "catechesis is necessary both for the maturation of the faith of Christians and for their witness in the world" (*CT* 25). Therefore, "there is no separation or opposition between catechesis and evangelization" (*CT* 18). The various elements of evangelization: "the renewal of humanity, witness, explicit proclamation, inner adherence, entry into the community, acceptance of signs, apostolic initiative" (*EN* 24) "are integral aspects of the process of catechesis."[12] The more people engage in African-American storytelling, the more people will understand their role in evangelization as living the Christian life. "Evangeli[zing] has to become more of a lifestyle than just an outreach or an event. . . . [I]t needs to be modeled and encouraged among the leaders and the rest of the church family."[13] Once this lifestyle is embraced, people will seek better relationships with one another, and the kin-dom of God builds.

FAITH FORMATION

Adult faith formation both evangelizes and catechizes adults. Called through my story which reflects the faith stories of old, your story comes to new life. The process of evangelization, awakening another to the word of God, moves into catechesis which "resounds" that word through tradition. *My Story-Your Story* then continues the process of faith formation. "We learn about our faith and what can be possible for us in our spiritual lives from hearing what others have to say about what God is doing. . . . Hearing what others say helps us see some of the possibilities that exist for us."[14]

Throughout Jesus's ministry and on through his passion to resurrection, we find Jesus focusing his attention on adults. Jesus's method met people in their circumstance and allowed them to tell their story before telling them his (Luke 24:13–35). This story of catechesis highlights adult faith formation as a necessary stone placed upon the cornerstone of Jesus in the building up of God's kin-dom. "The specific character of catechesis, as distinct from the initial conversion—bringing proclamation of the Gospel, has the twofold objective of maturing the initial faith and of educating the true disciple of Christ by means of a deeper and more systematic knowledge of the person and the message of our Lord Jesus Christ" (*CT* 19).

Jane Regan argues that "fostering the faith of the adults within a commu-nity has the effect of creating a context that supports the life of faith of every-one in the community."[15] In other words, ongoing adult faith formation helps create a community in which all its members are ordered in Christ. When households converted to Christ through the teaching and preaching of Paul, it was accomplished through the beliefs of the adults. The Church's early catechumenate was also structured for adults. "When people are linked to God's unfolding story, their own lives become different. Significant changes take place. People find that life has directions for them, that they have value as human beings."[16] Adults then are front runners helping to bring about the Reign of God.

When we look at adults as kin-dom builders, we realize that a fundamental aspect of faith formation is to help people learn to live the faith they profess. Adult faith formation that helps, "to put people not only in touch, but also in communion and intimacy, with Jesus Christ" (*GDC* 80), must be ongoing. It is ongoing because our faith is rooted in experience and experiences are always changing, ever new. Our experiences must continuously be placed under the light of the gospel in order that our future experiences/actions may be shaped by Christ. "So what we are about in catechesis is conversion and entering into a discipleship that lasts a lifetime and calls for continuing formation and transformation in terms of ongoing catechesis."[17]

African-American storytelling reminds us to hope in the ever-present God in an ever-changing world, opening our hearts to the understanding that we all indeed matter. Faith formation begins with each person discovering their value in God. Through the use of African-American storytelling, all generations situate their story in the Story. "Every time a story is told there is a meaning. No matter how many times you hear a story, there is something else in there. There is a return, something new that is given back, something stirred by the teller, something touched in the listener. We learn by listening, over and over again, like praying. . . . The power of the story is in the faith of those who speak and those who hear."[18] Just as audiences are not passive when traditional storytelling takes place, intergenerational faith formation must not render us passive. By using African-American storytelling as a method of catechesis, all generations will be fully engaged in learning our faith.

THEOLOGICAL REFLECTION

Growing in faith requires that we look critically at our lives in light of the gospel truth. Theological reflection helps us move our intimate and personal relationship with Jesus into a concrete lived experience. To better understand how this is done, I first define theological reflection then offer a model and method[19] for it. C. Vanessa White explains, "theological reflection is the ability to bring the Christian tradition into fruitful dialogue with contemporary experience, the goal being both to interpret the experience so as to see God's action in our world, God acting in us, and to formulate an adequate pastoral response to a situation in light of the tradition."[20]

The three major components to this model are experience, culture, and tradition. White states that when all three components converge within a storytelling methodology, the individual gains insight which then results in conversion.[21]

While insight helps the individual tell his/her story, it also gives her/him insight. Therefore, it is the engagement that is the doorway for conversion. White brings the components into dialogue using a six-step method that revolves around a theme. The six steps are storytelling, introduction of scripture, introduction from Catholic Tradition, cultural engagement, insights, and transformed response. The first step in the method engages experience where each person shares a personal story that examines the theme. It is here that the *My Story-Your Story* exchange begins. Once participants have shared in one another's stories, the movement is to the tradition component of the model. Scripture and Catholic Tradition are introduced. The questions asked about the scripture and Catholic Tradition are intended to help participants make scripture personal. "How does the scripture/Tradition connect with your story? How does it challenge and/or affirm your story?" Kenneth Hill

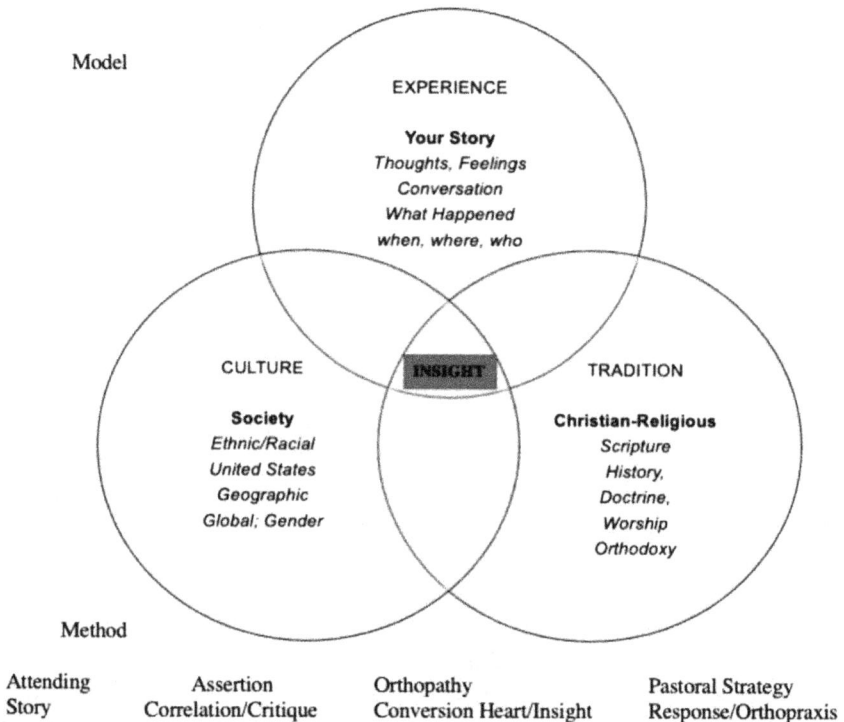

Model

EXPERIENCE

Your Story
Thoughts, Feelings
Conversation
What Happened
when, where, who

CULTURE

Society
Ethnic/Racial
United States
Geographic
Global; Gender

INSIGHT

TRADITION

Christian-Religious
Scripture
History,
Doctrine,
Worship
Orthodoxy

Method

| Attending | Assertion | Orthopathy | Pastoral Strategy |
| Story | Correlation/Critique | Conversion Heart/Insight | Response/Orthopraxis |

Figure 3.1 Adapted from Whitehead Method in Method in Ministry and Copeland, Phelps, Eugene Black Theology Method in Taking Down Our Harps

states that scripture underscores oral tradition that is "reechoed" in order to foster faith.[22]

The next step in White's method, step four, asks participants to engage their culture,[23] the third component in the model. At this point, having engaged experience, tradition, and culture, participants are asked to do a critical analysis to gain insight into their own story. These insights are shared in the community, reinforcing the *My Story-Your Story* connection. The final step, transformed response, calls the participants to discern the action God is calling them to do.

This storytelling of people of faith opens the door on people's experiences of God which is important to me because effective catechesis/faith formation begins with each person's story. Culture determines how the experiences will be conveyed, while scripture/Tradition is where the educator brings in the Christian story. Critical analysis is the dialogue each person has with his or her life story, culture, and the Christian scripture/Tradition in order to gain insight and formulate a response. This model and method moves in unison with Thomas Groome's "Shared Christian Praxis" outlined later in the chapter.

THEOLOGICAL REFLECTION AND CATECHESIS

While catechesis provides for the teaching of the faith via its various modes, theological reflection allows for that teaching to be broken open onto the lives of the participants. Theological reflection pulls the subject matter of catechesis into people's lived experience, while catechesis keeps theological reflection from being just one person's story. It requires people to place their story into the larger context of the Church's story. "Traditional storytelling is incomplete and even meaningless without practical participation by both the narrator and the audience."[24] This dialogical activity takes place through theological reflection. Theological reflection allows the story to not only be told but also be interacted with.

When we look at the "fundamental tasks of catechesis: promoting knowledge of faith; liturgical education; moral formation; missionary invitation" (*GDC* 85), we must acknowledge that theological reflection is a key component. Briefly put, catechesis requires theological reflection in order for conversion to occur. The two together transform both the heart and mind (*GDC* 55).

The one message—the Good News of salvation—that has been heard once or hundreds of times and has been accepted with the heart, is in catechesis probed unceasingly by reflection and systematic study, by awareness of its repercussions on one's personal life—an awareness calling for ever greater commitment—and by inserting it into an organic and harmonious whole, namely, Christian living in society and the world. (*CT* 26)

Together, catechesis and theological reflection can help cultivate a prayer life that may expand beyond one's personal relationship with Jesus Christ into the shared worship of God in liturgies that may lead to communal expression in daily living. "From the oral teaching by the apostles and the letters circulating among the churches down to the most modern means, catechesis has not ceased to look for the most suitable ways and means for its mission, with the active participation of the communities and at the urging of the pastors. This effort must continue" (*CT* 46).

STORYING THE FAITH

One of my favorite things about visiting a Protestant Church is the testimony[25] part of the service, when people get up and tell the congregation about "What the Lord has done for me." When people share their stories of God acting in their lives, storying the faith happens. We need places in the Catholic Church to tell and hear testimonies. In storying the faith, it will be necessary to take notice of everyone's experiences and help them see how their story is part of the "old, old Story." "One of the greatest gifts of the Church is age. As the centuries have unfolded, we the Church have learned much about what it means to be saved. So we can tell this old, old Story. Yet each generation and culture retells the Story with a distinction and a freshness because each has experienced the Story somewhat differently."[26] It is because of this distinction that intergenerational catechesis is the next step in faith formation for the Catholic Church.

STORYTELLING AND CATECHESIS

My Story-Your Story and the Story

My Story-Your Story speaks of our connection through story. When I tell my story you find a point in which to intersect, connecting your story to mine. Our linkage invites us to see ourselves and one another differently. We are better able to see our union in God because "stories invite [us] into a realm of possibility in which [we] may learn new ways of being faithful people in the world."[27] "My story is wrapped up in your story, and it is God's Story."[28] As faithful people, we realize that "at the heart of our Christian faith is a story. And at the heart of [catechesis] must be this same story. When we evaluate our corporate lives as a community of faith, this story must judge us. Our ritual life, the experiences we have in community, and the acts we perform in the world, must be informed by this story. Unless the story is known, understood, owned, and lived, [we] will not have [Catholic] faith."[29]

Through *My Story-Your Story*, we see clearer how "all stories serve that one story, and all tellers serve the universal word that invites us and demands that we become truly human and divine."[30] This one Story has been passed down from generation to generation, first orally, then in written format, becoming the bible, the sacred writings of God acting in and through ordinary and extraordinary people, from the poor to the wealthy, famous to infamous.[31] Though it is one Story, it is the compilation of many stories, composed by various authors, witnesses of God's revelation, in the form of prayers, songs, epics, prose, laws, letters, poetry, and visions/dreams. "The Bible is at the center of Christian education. This centrality arises from the Christian church's basis in the story. The story of God's love is made known in creation, in redemption through the people of Israel, and through the life, death, and resurrection of Jesus Christ. As Christians, everyone participates in this story."[32] African-American storytelling makes it possible for catechists to better help us understand this truth and see ourselves in it.

For us who embrace the Christian Story as meaningful, our participation in the Story is "a movement from that which is seen and heard and felt to the God who, through them, opens us more to divine encounter, using the whole of our experience to draw us closer if we are open, hospitable, receptive."[33] We live the story of this participation in and through our words and deeds.

The Intersection of story and Story

Thomas Groome's shared Christian praxis approach presents a framework for catechesis in which story plays a significant part. It is significant in that it makes room for African-American storytelling to take place in several of its movements. There are five movements in Groome's framework: present action, critical reflection, Christian Story and Vision, the Story and participants' stories, and the Vision and participants' visions.[34] In this framework, story begins in the first movement. "Present action is whatever way we give expression to ourselves."[35] *My Story-Your Story* comes to life in this movement by allowing the teller and listener to find connectedness in their stories, which are then nuanced throughout the framework. Groome's second movement, critical reflection, is the point in which theological reflection occurs. Using C. Vanessa White's model of theological reflection, *My Story-Your Story* calls for reflection on experience, tradition, and culture in order to move it into dialogue with the Story.

The third movement, the Christian Story and Vision, is "the whole faith tradition of our people however that is expressed or embodied. . . . Remembering and representing the Story is an essential part of the Jewish and Christian process of knowing God. . . . We experience salvation for our time by remembering and reencountering the Story of God's savings deeds."[36] The Story, therefore, is retold in order for us to find our place and reorient our lives. Luke 24:13–35 is the story of two men journeying to Emmaus. This story illustrates how Jesus meets us where we are, listens to our story, and reminds us of the larger Story, before helping us find our place in it. This retelling of the Story is important in that it brings us to an understanding of Christian faith beyond the personal relationship with Jesus (*GDC* 144). As Nathan Jones explains:

> This living Story is not something you organize and plan to tell and re-tell, but it is something you feel, something which gives life, which motivates and urges you onward. Furthermore, the Story gives you just what you need in order to deal with life's struggles, hardships, and questions. This Story is *your* Story. It is not just a story that has been passed on by tradition, parents, a priest or a sister. It is a Story you have gratefully claimed as your own. It is an old Story interpreted for a new day.[37]

The new interpretation of the Story helps move us beyond our personal relationship with Jesus into the community, which strengthens not only the person but also the community in a way that transforms it into God's kin-dom.

The fourth movement in Groome's shared Christian praxis approach, the Story and participants' stories, invites the return to theological reflection, where we are helped to see the various aspects of our story and that of the Christian community. Here African-American storytelling uplifts experience and uses it to teach truths that may otherwise be overlooked. These stories are not too different from biblical stories that recount the movement of God. "The Bible, as a teaching source, illuminates the mind, moves the heart, and stirs the soul."[38] It tells the story of God acting in people's lives and people's responses to that action. "The story in scripture, told in and through the church, shapes our understanding of reality. The scriptures provide a grid or set of images by which we may come to believe and interpret our own life experiences."[39] For it is in and through story that we discover not just facts, but the incarnate God. Megan McKenna and Tony Cowan elaborate:

> The Christian tradition proclaims that The Word became Flesh and dwells among us. In response we, with our words of belief, of assent, of shared hope, must become flesh for others' food. Our flesh must bear witness to the presence of words instilled and cherished, believed and borne witness to in commitment,

example and service, and sometimes in the giving of life itself as the final word. It is still the best story, the only story worth telling.[40]

African-American storytelling harnesses this concept. It brings to life the faith of peoples who struggle to grow in faith and love of God and others. "Telling and retelling stories from the Bible, from our faith communities, and from our everyday lives as people of faith evokes concrete images and memories that propel us into imaginatively recreating our village connections."[41] Once these connections are re-imaged, we move into action, we respond.

The fifth and last movement, the Vision and participants' visions, calls for a response or as White states in her model, a "transformed" response. The stories shared and reflected upon help people see the future action they should take. "We live our lives immersed in stories. [W]hile some stories entertain, inform, or teach us, others move us deeply. They change us and bring us closer together. These are sacred stories. [S]acred stories . . . tell us 'who we are and how we relate to the world and our gods.' "[42] These stories "suggest ways to motivate people to action, help them see themselves in a new light, help them recognize new resources, enable them to channel behavior in constructive ways, sustain them in crises, bring healing and reconciliation in relationships, heal the scars of memories, and provide guidance when direction is needed."[43]

Groome's shared Christian praxis approach helps us see the importance of the communal aspect of religion through which we are called to speak aloud our faith stories. "The oral tradition itself tells a story of the precariousness of words, events and experiences. It conveys knowledge long before that knowledge has been recorded, whether on skins and pictures or in the words of one's native tongue or a second language. The story, like the people in it, lives."[44]

It is through story that one is better able to understand God at work in the world. "Stories taught African Americans how to respond to their abilities (that is, responsibilities), even if this was no more than utilizing their gift for memory and an innate understanding of the situations that confronted them."[45] *My Story-Your Story* is the discovery of God's saving mercy at work in and through us that will teach us how to share our abilities/responsibilities.

Storytellers

Though all of us who share a story, *My Story-Your Story*, are storytellers, I highlight three storytellers that play an important role in this dialogue by displaying how each has sought to keep their audiences aware of the world around them and uplift them in a way that helps them shake off various oppressive situations. These storytellers are rapper/emcee, preacher, and catechist.

The first of these storytellers is the rapper/emcee. The rapper/emcee is the voice of the hip-hop culture, which as "a subculture of urban culture, its influence has spread beyond the confines of the city. It has risen from its inner-city roots to influence youth from the American suburbs to Tokyo. As the top consumers of its music, white teenage males in America do a great job of keeping the hip-hop culture in business."[46] The rapper/emcee is able to express the fears, joys and sorrows of young adults in a gritty way that lends itself to the realism of their actual experiences. This ability to make experiences come to life is what cuts across cultural borders.

The rapper/emcee is so influential because of the power of words to transform. "The emcee can choose to use their gifts and knowledge in a way that educates and uplifts the listener or degrades and downgrades the listener."[47] Young adults influenced by the emcee are drawn into the rapper's ability to tell a story about their experiences. Through the lyrics, the rapper speaks about situations and/or circumstances to which many young adults are able to connect. "Hip-hop has used rap to tell stories of urban youth, poverty, oppression, inner-city life, anger and African American history."[48] With storytelling being used so extensively among young adults, the use of it in intergenerational catechesis is a natural progression.

The rapper/emcee as catechist is a leap that must be made when you consider their storytelling abilities because "through the emcee you learn the history, culture, philosophies and doctrines of hip-hop."[49] As an emcee-catechist, the lyrics are no longer just about young adult hip-hop culture but the joys, sorrows, fears of all of us in relation to the Story.

The second storyteller is the preacher. The preacher draws upon experiences of the past to tell stories for use in the present. When the preacher is "good" (a subjective term), the stories told will allow the hearers to see the scripture passage he exegeted in a new way, in a way that makes sense for our lives. "The biblical story itself enables the preacher to interpret God's saving Word in light of the lived experiences, struggles, and strides of the people."[50] The preacher's use of story during the sermon "provide[s] connections between the present and the past, to study and explain the past within the context of the present, and vice versa."[51] The preacher then is expected to use the pulpit as "an educational place where its members not only [learn] spiritual truths but also how to apply them to everyday life."[52] Preaching, like story, uses the imagination. "Just as visual images must conform to the people, to diminish the distance between those people and their God, so must the ear images conform."[53] The preacher can be seen as an intergenerational storyteller since he is to address all who are in attendance.

The catechists, the third storyteller, often seen only as religious educators, are persons who assist the Church with ongoing faith formation. Intergenerational catechesis demands that we move beyond the traditional view of catechists as religious educators to include all roles and ministries where people are formed in faith. In this role, catechists are not only storytellers; they are also facilitators of story. African-American storytelling provides the foundation upon which each person is able to build their story of faith and then join it with the Church, the People of God, the Body of Christ.

Returning to Groome's shared Christian praxis we find that the movements must be facilitated in order to engage people. The catechist, therefore, begins the movements as a facilitator, becoming a storyteller by the third movement when the Story is introduced. The dual role of the catechist affords the catechist some flexibility in sharing the Story. The catechist becomes more like the African griot, who "supplies memory and cultural direction to all people involved in ritual performance."[54] The catechist, when using African-American storytelling, provides the hearer with the memories of our Catholic faith, reminding us how we are to live, thereby calling us to Christian living. Like Jesus in the Emmaus Story, the catechist recounts the biblical story on which the formation session is centered. Though we don't like to think of catechesis as performance, we must broaden our thinking to include African-American storytelling and how its performative use educates—for "the oral process . . . is a legitimate system of teaching and learning[.]"[55]

When the storyteller has finished telling the story, "the story has not ended. The audience has taken it home with them, and the next day they spread the word to the ones who were not there to witness the event."[56] When scripture is proclaimed in a liturgy, we tell the story of God intending that the hearers take the word with them in order to evangelize the absent. "The act of telling a story is a ritual. It seeks to transmit knowledge and pass on secrets of the heart and soul cherished by a community of people. It opens those who hear, who copy the stories and try to tell them, interpreting the secrets of the God that this community believes in and follows."[57]

St. Paul reminds us that faith comes through the hearing of the word. African-American storytelling focuses on spoken word that allows person to reach person. It moves us beyond the superficial, the ideological, the theory, into the practical, the living of life. Storytellers help us remember ancient truths that must be kept alive. "The events of the past are never sealed. Story provides insight but never closure."[58] The Paschal Mystery of Jesus is the ancient Story retold so that Christians remember the truth of God's saving grace.

The African-American Church Experience

In the previous section, I highlighted the preacher as storyteller. Looking at preaching then through a catechetical lens, it is imperative that Roman Catholic preaching, taking a cue from African-American worship, seek to become relevant in the lives of the People of God. "Black preaching and black worship have established traditions centered in nurturing black wholeness and empowerment for living under oppressive conditions. The preaching task has focused on interpreting biblical Christianity in the interests of black humanity and faith development in black life."[59] This way of addressing the needs of African-Americans is necessary also for the Catholic Church in regards to people who are suffering. African-American storytelling aids the preacher here in crafting sermons that not only contain the content of importance but also the delivery. Call-and-response, one of the African-American preaching styles employed by preachers in many African-American churches, helps individuals place their own story within the Story, thereby, achieving wholeness and empowerment. It is important to note that wholeness is not just for the individual. Wholeness "includes healing amid sustaining and guiding, and the reconciliation of humanity to God, to self and to each other[.]"[60]

In many African-American churches, there exists a focus on "nurturing[61] the black person, teaching coping skills and self-worth, and empower[ing] one to seek fullness of life. It [also] addresses the search for meaning and value of life in relation to God and neighbor."[62] In our quest for wholeness and belonging, each of us need the stories of others in addition to the Story in order to grow and find meaning that opens us more fully to God and others. Scripture tells the Story in which we discover our Christian identity. For "Christianity is seen most effectively through the interpretations of meaning and identity derived from Scripture. Therefore, in the formation and agency of black churches, preaching thrives at the center of worship and the communal experience of pastoral care."[63] Preaching in the context of worship takes us back to storytelling and its importance in our lives.

The nurturing that takes place in many African-American worship services is the same nurturing that needs to take place for us to continue growing in faith. African-American "worship makes possible discernment through life's opportunities and its darkness."[64] This discernment process is not to be passive. Because it is about growth, there will be "growing pains" that call for adjustment. This nurturing is like a dialogue that will ask us to not just be passive, but to be active in the process. "To make a difference in our lives, nurture must arouse not just the something, but the 'more' that brings an awareness, a discernment, even a struggling with the effects of nurture or what is being cultivated in us."[65]

Many of us, like African-Americans, are looking

for a deepening faith and an alive hope that is more than an individualistic orientation to faith and hope. There is a search for a communally shared or "village" faith and hope that evokes in persons a zeal to make faith and hope concretely felt in and beyond the congregation through actions intended to make a better world.[66]

The African-American experience of church thereby calls for an integration of the congregation's story with the Story, not just for the individual, but also for the entire church. Storytelling within this context helps shape the future by allowing hope to be heard when it cannot always be seen.

The Catechist and African-American Storytelling

African-American storytelling is an indispensable catechetical method because "there is a world of difference between reading and hearing a story."[67] This method moves beyond memorization into the world of the person. *My Story-Your Story* becomes the foci, where people enter more fully into the understanding that all persons are not only important but also connected.

> In general, the oral tradition is stronger and truer, deeper and more meaningful than any written tradition because of its origins in the community. The written traditions, such as scriptures . . . are inspired. The depth of meanings veiled and hidden in the text and its spaces demands that that the reader, the hearer, and then eventually the teller dig down deep to discover and reveal the heart of the message and serve it religiously and devotedly.[68]

In reaching deeper into stories, both oral and written, we discover that "stories are crucial to our sense of well-being, to identity, to memory, and to our future."[69] We understand better how "stories save our lives on basic levels and on levels of great subtlety and depth."[70] Story, then, teaches us how to be in relationship with one another. Through story we recapture our connection to other, better understanding our role in community.[71]

African-American storytelling "enabled African Americans to survive in a culture that denied us the right to define our own value and worth as human beings. Thus . . . African American storytelling is an artistic and imaginative practice of meaning-making that, although derived from necessity, focused on God's presence."[72] Since different groups are finding themselves all too often marginalized like African-Americans, African-American storytelling will allow us to better learn the Catholic faith.

> A [catechist] who understands the working of God through drama can link people with the unfolding of God's story. Such a [person] seeks to help parishioners

develop story language and story discernment in order to visualize how God's drama is unfolding in their lives. This means that telling and listening to stories become central to the caring process. It also means that people learn to follow the plots of stories, to visualize how God is seeking to engage them in the drama as it affects their lives.[73]

The telling and listening aspect of African-American storytelling affords catechists the tools necessary to better assist the People of God in learning the faith.

> Story—storytelling and listening—is a central methodology of catechetical ministry. Story is not simply a passing, present-day interest of the religious community, but rather an attempt to recover a lost emphasis. Christian faith did not originally come to us as theology. The Good News came to us as story: "In the beginning . . ." As the ages have unfolded, this Story has become a cherished tradition handed on down the generations with care.[74]

Storytelling based on the relationship between storyteller and listener moves away from the individualism often called for in society toward community which is church. "Like the Afrikangriot, catechists are ministers of the community's story. . . . [T]he catechist, like Jesus, invites his/her people to see their dying and rising in relationship to the dying and rising of Jesus. Therefore, the catechist . . . must speak to the hearts of the people like a poet, an elder, someone who loves them dearly."[75] Scripture is the oral stories of faith written for memory's sake and brought to life again when proclaimed in liturgies, when studied in groups and in private, and when retold for the purposes of education.

> The process of storytelling involves hearing a story told and making it your own, telling it yourself and then passing it on according to age-old accepted rules and disciplines. The story is passed on from one mouth to another, being transferred to paper only in a shorthand form for memory's sake, or to make the story more singular or detailed in a different form: that of writing.[76]

By using African-American storytelling to catechize, catechists become narrators opening people to the words, ideas, and practices of the Catholic faith. "In the process of storytelling, the narrator makes use of words that are from the womb of tradition, thereby educating the children in the language of their people."[77] When the narrator uses images and situations familiar to one generation and not the other, he/she creates moments for the generations to interact—to enter into the story and share in the teaching.

In this chapter, I highlighted how each of us are storytellers when we share our story. By lifting up the rapper/emcee, the preacher, and the catechist as storytellers, I showed how story permeates our living, setting us free in the Story. I discussed how storytelling accompanies ongoing faith formation and illustrated the bond between evangelization and catechesis in the effort to show how they cannot be separated from one another. The discussion on theological reflection depicted the role African-American storytelling plays in storying the faith. African-American storytelling as a method of catechesis opens us more fully to God and others, enabling us to value testifying as a way to "help [us] remember who [we] are, help [us] make the common stories and symbols of faith [our] own, and help [us] enrich [our] heritage with special meaning for [our] own lives and times."[78]

NOTES

1. Kenneth H. Hill, *Religious Education in the African American Tradition: A Comprehensive Introduction* (St. Louis: Chalice Press, 2007), 40–41.

2. Groome, *Christian Religious Education: Sharing Our Story and Vision*, 149.

3. Groome, *Christian Religious Education: Sharing Our Story and Vision*, 26.

4. Throughout the gospels are stories of Jesus healing people of faith. One such story is that of the hemorrhaging woman, Luke 8:44–47.

5. Toinette Eugene, "Christian Education: A Ministry of the Word," in *Tell It Like It Is: A Black Catholic Perspective on Christian Education,*ed. Eva Marie Lumas (Oakland: National Black Sisters' Conference, 1983), 4.

6. Eugene, 7–8.

7. John Paul II, "The Apostolic Exhortation on Catechesis in Our Time *CatechesiTradendae* (1979),"in *The Catechetical Documents: A Parish Resource*(Chicago: Liturgy Training Publications, 1996), 375–416, no. 20. Subsequent references will be made parenthetically citing *CT*.

8. Jones, 20.

9. Robert J. Hater, *The Relationship Between Evangelization and Catechesis* (Washington, DC: National Conference of Diocesan Directors of Religious Education, 1981), 5.

10. Hater, 6.

11. John H. Westerhoff, III, *Will Our Children Have Faith?*(New York: The Seabury Press, 1976), 88.

12. Catherine Dooley, "Evangelization and Catechesis: Partners for a New Millennium," in *The Echo Within: Emerging Issues in Religious Education*, eds. Catherine Dooley and Mary Collins (Allen, TX: Thomas More, 1997), 152.

13. Tommy Kyllonen, *Un.orthodox: Church, Hip-Hop, Culture* (Grand Rapids, MI: Zondervan, 2007), 142.

14. Edward P. Wimberly, *Moving From Shame to Self-Worth: Preaching and Pastoral Care* (Nashville: Abingdon Press, 1999), 13.

15. Jane E. Regan, *Toward an Adult Church: A Vision of Faith Formation* (Chicago: Loyola Press, 2002), 11.

16. Edward P. Wimberly, *African American Pastoral Care*,rev. ed. (Nashville: Abingdon Press, 2008), 5.

17. Jane E. Regan, "The Aim of Catechesis," in *Horizons and Hopes: The Future of Religious Education*, ed. Thomas H. Groome and Harold Daly Horell (New York/ Mahwah, NJ: Paulist Press, 2003), 36.

18. McKenna and Cowan, 81.

19. C. Vanessa White, Associate Professor of Spirituality and Ministry at Catholic Theological Union is working on this model at the Institute for Black Catholic Studies at Xavier University of LA. The model is entitled "Spirit and Story: An Emerging Model/Method of Theological Reflection."

20. In defining theological reflection, White acknowledges those who came before her who she used to further her own understanding of method—particularly James and Evelyn Whitehead, David Poling, Patricia Killen and John de Beer. She developed this method and model because she sensed their methods were not working for her community. While she acknowledges that all theological reflection methods look at culture, experience and tradition, her distinction is in how she defines those terms and how she engages them within the context of a storytelling methodology. Phone interview April 9, 2011. Her use of storytelling underscores the importance of story in faith formation.

21. See Figure 3.1: Illustration of C. Vanessa White's emerging model/method.

22. Hill, 57.

23. My understanding of culture is the situations and circumstances that make up one's present life. See Stephen B. Bevans, *Models of Contextual Theology: Faith and Cultures*,rev.ed. (Maryknoll, NY: Orbis Books, 2002), 5.

24. BayoOgunjimi and Abdul-Rasheed Na'Allah, *Introduction to African Oral Literature and Performance* (Trenton, NJ: Africa World Press, Inc., 2005), 22.

25. Merriam-Webster, "A Public Expression of Religious Experience," accessed March 4, 2020, http://www.merriam-webster.com/dictionary/testimony.

26. Jones, 7.

27. Susan M. Shaw, *Storytelling in Religious Education* (Birmingham, AL: Religious Education Press, 1999), xi.

28. Jones, 8.

29. Westerhoff, III, 34.

30. McKenna and Cowan, 177.

31. Paul VI, "Dogmatic Constitution on Divine Revelation,"*Dei Verbum*, 1965, no. 3, accessed March 4, 2020, http://www.vatican.va/archive/hist_councils/ii_vatican_council/documents/vat-ii_const_19651118_dei-verbum_en.html

32. Hill, 39.

33. Kathleen Hughes, *Saying Amen: A Mystagogy of Sacrament* (Chicago: Liturgy Training Publications, 1999), 27.

34. Groome, *Christian Religious Education: Sharing Our Story and Vision*,184.

35. Groome, *Christian Religious Education: Sharing Our Story and Vision*,184.

36. Groome, *Christian Religious Education: Sharing Our Story and Vision*,192.

37. Jones, 74.

38. Hill, 28.

39. Hill, 40.

40. McKenna and Cowan, 203.

41. Wimberly, *African American Pastoral Care*,x.

42. Charles and Anne Simpkinson, eds.,*Sacred Stories: A Celebration of the Power of Story to Transform and Heal* (San Francisco: Harper San Francisco, 1993), 1.

43. Wimberly, *African American Pastoral Care*, 3.

44. McKenna and Cowan, 138.

45. D'JimoKouyate, "The Role of the Griot," in *Talk That Talk: An Anthology of African-American Storytelling*, eds. Linda Goss and Marian E. Barnes (New York: Simon and Schuster, 1989), 215–216.

46. Efrem Smith and Phil Jackson, *The Hip-Hop Church*(Downers Grove: InterVarsity Press, 2005), 105.

47. Smith and Jackson, 155.

48. Smith and Jackson, 112.

49. Smith and Jackson, 153–154.

50. Jones, 65.

51. Scheub, 13.

52. D'JimoKouyate, "The Role of the Griot," in *Talk That Talk: An Anthology of African-American Storytelling*, eds.Linda Goss and Marian E. Barnes (New York: Simon and Schuster, 1989), 215.

53. Henry H. Mitchell, "Black Preaching," in *Black Church Lifestyles: Rediscovering the Black Christian Experience*, compiler Emmanuel L. McCall(Nashville: Broadman Press, 1986), 121.

54. Ogunjimi and Na'Allah, xiii.

55. Ella Mitchell, "Black Nurture," in *Black Church Lifestyles: Rediscovering the Black Christian Experience*, compiler Emmanuel L. McCall(Nashville: Broadman Press, 1986), 50.

56. Goss and Barnes, 11.

57. McKenna and Cowan, 64.

58. Scheub, 3.

59. Andrews, 23.

60. Andrews, 29.

61. My use of nurture is based on Anne StreatyWimberly, *Nurturing Faith and Hope: Black Worship as a Model for Christian Education* (Cleveland: The Pilgrim Press, 2004), xiii–xv, where she states that nurture is akin to cultivating whereas plant life would not grow if it is not nourish/cultivated.

62. Andrews, 40.

63. Andrews, 40.

64. Anne StreatyWimberly, *Nurturing Faith and Hope: Black Worship as a Model for Christian Education* (Cleveland: The Pilgrim Press, 2004), xiii.

65. Wimberly, *Nurturing Faith and Hope: Black Worship as a Model for Christian Education*,xiv.

66. Wimberly, *Nurturing Faith and Hope: Black Worship as a Model for Christian Education*, xvii–xviii.

67. McKenna and Cowan, 175.
68. McKenna and Cowan, 176.
69. McKenna and Cowan, 196.
70. McKenna and Cowan, 196.
71. Westerhoff, III, 19.
72. Wimberly, *African American Pastoral Care*, xi–xii.
73. Wimberly, *African American Pastoral Care*, 6.
74. Jones, 7.
75. Jones, 79.
76. McKenna and Cowan, 174.
77. Ogunjimi and Na'Allah, 22.
78. Hill, 26.

Chapter 4

Healing and Story

Faith Formation, Trauma, and Violence

Now the earth was corrupt in God's sight, and the earth was filled with violence. And God saw that the earth was corrupt; for all flesh had corrupted its ways upon the earth.

—Genesis 6:11–12

Faith formation usually brings to mind God's love for us and our love for God, self, and others. It speaks of our willingness to share the good news of Jesus Christ, while we are growing and transforming into better followers of Jesus. Yet, for us Christ-followers, trauma and violence are a part of our faith. In Genesis, Adam and Eve experience trauma when they are ejected from the garden of Eden to face the violence of a new environment.[1] COVID-19 has infused us with trauma in ways that we are still unpacking. The passion narratives of Jesus tell of his suffering and ultimately his murder at the hands of the Romans, instigated by Jewish leaders.[2] Recounting the passion narratives each year at the end of the Lenten Season to prepare us for the joys of Jesus's resurrection is faith formation rooted in love that moves through trauma and violence. I don't want to confuse love with trauma and violence, but I do want to point out that faith formation is connected to stories of trauma and violence and therefore must be addressed.

This look into trauma and violence is important to understanding generational interactions. This is not to say that all generational interactions are traumatic, but it is commonly understood that as one generation transitions to the next, there exists perceived wrongs and misunderstandings that can be traumatic and even violent, that is, the movement of one generation living under Jim Crow laws to another fighting for civil rights to another not understanding what all the fuss is about. For intergenerational catechesis to be effective, we must recognize that there exists pains and agonies unique to each generation and also passed down through generations—inherited trauma.

> Events carry within them and "pass on" from generation to generation a traumatic character, as if human beings were condemned to repeat the very events that traumatized persons and communities. Communities are condemned to repeat the violence of their origins, the violence that they, at one point in their history, committed or suffered.[3]

William S. Schmidt adds to this understanding of trauma, when he states that there needs to be more trauma resources that include theological and spiritual awareness "to truly be adequate for the challenges of deep and extended trauma narratives . . . , to hold the disintegration and alienation patterns of trauma with deep insight, and offer sufferers perhaps an even greater spiritual capacity to overcome their lived negation."[4]African-American storytelling brings to the forefront underlying and/or known traumas when it roots people's stories in the Story of Jesus. *My Story-Your Story* helps people articulate their narrative so that they are able to see the trauma and/or violence in a more objective way. Though I will not be delving into the psychology of trauma in this chapter, it is important to note that

> trauma interrupts the natural unfolding of the psyche, which inevitably leads to significant developmental effects. Particularly early life trauma, but even extended adult trauma is never erasable, since there is no clean slate to reach back for or reconstruct. There is no way to start over "fresh," so the only way forward includes having to come to terms with the trauma residue that keeps intruding into here and now eruptions, which threaten any gains one might make.[5]

Intergenerational catechesis that uses African-American storytelling helps us move away "from virtual contact to good and healthy communication" (*CV* 90) which foster the establishment of friendships that teach "us to be open, understanding and caring towards others, to come out of our own comfortable isolation and to share lives with others" (*CV* 151). This in turn revitalizes young people's interest in history while prompting older people to look toward the future. "When young and old alike are open to the Holy Spirit, they make a wonderful combination. The old dream dreams, and the young see visions" (*CV* 192). In this chapter I will discuss how story can help identify and then heal trauma and violence in the course of faith formation.

INTERGENERATIONAL AND HISTORICAL TRAUMA

Before beginning this project, I did not make distinctions between intergenerational trauma and historical trauma because I was only looking through the lens of one historical trauma, slavery. I have since discovered the difference and importance of making distinctions, although you will find that they can and often are collapsed upon each other. "Historical trauma is multigenerational trauma experienced by a specific cultural, racial or ethnic group. It is related to major events that oppressed a particular group of people because of their status as oppressed, such as slavery, the Holocaust, forced migration, and the violent colonization of Native Americans."[6] Intergenerational trauma is "any family trauma that wasn't dealt with appropriately at the time that results in a pattern of traumatic or unhealthy behaviors, beliefs, and/or attitudes transferred down to younger generations; a long lineage of unresolved emotions that result in biological, psychological and neurological changes."[7] Intergenerational trauma can be, and often is, influenced by historical trauma.

In chapter 2, I introduced intergenerational and historic trauma when I discussed the "ways of being" that my mother taught me as I was growing up. Many of her lessons came out of her childhood experience of living in Jim Crow segregated Birmingham, Alabama, while others are rooted in the segregation of Chicago in the 1940s and 1950s. Her experiences were passed on to her children in the stories she told to make sure we "stayed in line." "The concreteness of stories evokes the particulars of place and our attachments to them. They bring up feelings, desires, without losing the sense of place."[8] I found myself doing something similar with my son when he started driving without me being in the car. I told him, "If you get pulled over by the police, put the car in park and put your hands on the steering wheel and do not move them. If the officer asks for your driver's license and vehicle registration, inform him of their location before you move your hands. Do not! under any circumstances, move without first giving notice. Do not argue and make sure you get his badge number." Molly Castelloe affirms this passing on of trauma when she states,

[p]sychic legacies are often passed on through unconscious cues or affective messages that flow between adult and child. Sometimes anxiety falls from one generation to the next through stories told. . . . Transgenerational transmissions take on life in our dreams, in acting out, in "life lessons" given in turns of phrase and taught us by our family. The emotional ties between child and ancestors are essential to the development of our values. These bonds often determine the answers to myriad questions such as: "Who am I?" "Who am I to my family?" "Who can 'we' trust and who are our enemies?"[9]

As story shares people's history, customs, and values, we are able to get a clearer understanding of how trauma can be inherited. This reminds us that we are catechizing persons, members of families, each with their own story, each with their own inherited trauma. It is worth mentioning again here,

Henry Louis Gates's thoughts on story and the shaping of beliefs and values from chapter 2:

> The stories that we tell ourselves and our children function to order our world, serving to create both a foundation upon which each of us constructs our sense of reality and a filter through which we process each event that confronts us every day. The values that we cherish and wish to preserve, the behavior that we wish to censure, the fear and dread that we can barely confess in ordinary language, the aspirations and goals that we most dearly prize—all of these things are encoded in the stories that each culture invents and preserves for the next generation, stories that, in effect, we live by and through.[10]

COVID-19 is an example of both a historical trauma and an intergenerational trauma. It is historical in that it is affecting the world at once, cutting across boundaries such as race, gender, sexuality, ethnicity, and socioeconomic status. It is intergenerational in that all generations have been touched by the disease whether through social distancing and stay-at-home directives or by hearing about and/or knowing people who have died. African-American storytelling, with its roots in trauma, both historical and intergenerational, is equipped for leading people through their narratives by liberating people from what binds them.

HEALING MEMORY

I never really liked the idea of forgiveness until I discovered it was forgiveness that was holding me back from a fuller relationship with God. To me forgiveness was equivalent to forgetting and forgetting was not an option. What I have since learned about forgiveness is that

> [w]e do not forget; we remember in a different way. The "forgetting" that we do in forgiving is an overcoming of anger and resentment, a being freed from the entanglements of those emotions and their capacity to keep us bound to an event.[11]

How gratifying it was to learn that I could be set free; to know that "human forgiveness . . . is deciding for a different future. It does not mean ignoring or forgetting the past. To ignore or forget the past is to demean the victim, trivialize the suffering that the victim has undergone."[12] Forgiveness as part of the process of reconciliation, in the Christian framework, is often spoken of as an action that God initiates on our behalf. "Ultimately, reconciliation is not a human achievement, but the work of God within us . . . [initiated] . . . in the lives of the victims."[13] We are able to enter into the process of reconciliation therefore, because of our relationship with God who freely gives us God's self in Jesus Christ, showing us how we are to be with others, reconciled.

Forgiveness then is about being in right relationship, with God, self, and others, though self is often overlooked. Nathan Jones puts into perspective how our individual struggles affect the community and the healing effects of storytelling:

> Denial and rejection of one's life-story touches not only persons alienated from our churches but also members of our local congregations. Many of us, too, are not at home with our pasts. There are many wounds, psychological scars, harsh and unfriendly memories that we would prefer to forget. Sometimes the pain is too much to uncover again. Lifting up my burdens to God is healing. To speak my pains and fears in a trusting community is healing. When I freely share my weaknesses with others I know and trust, these weaknesses can be transformed into strengths and power for new life. Testifying has been a tradition of the Black church in the United States and as religious educators we can gain much by discovering the richness of this communal storytelling experience.[14]

What becomes clear is that forgiveness is not a one-time thing but an ongoing process that teaches us how to live. "There is no past tense to forgiveness. . . . Each day has to be a renewal of our decision to forgive, because we face the jagged edges of our world every single day."[15] "Forgiveness, then, is both a process and a decision to act."[16]

With emotion being a key element in story it is important to keep in mind that story also draws upon the memories of both the storyteller and the listener.

> Story has always been used to provide connections between the present and the past, to study and explain the past within the context of the present, and vice versa . . . Story [then] is an artful mixing of images by means of pattern, drawing on the working within two contexts, the past and the present. Images from the past typically have an emotional content, or the capacity and the character to elicit emotions when brought into contact with contemporary, more realistic images.[17]

Since memory is a key component to storytelling it is important that the healing of memories be explored to prepare people to tell their story. In this time of instant information, easy access, and experience as much as you can as soon as you can, many people are left with feelings of guilt, anger, remorse, and shame that hinder their faith formation in addition to their involvement in Church. Thinking that earthly punishment is the best way to God's glory, many of us allow our past escapades to hinder and sometimes prevent our growth in faith. "The force of storytelling depends not simply on the surface facets of the story but on experiences . . . on memories that resonate and echo through the experiences of the members of the audience, and on the immediacy of contemporary references in the story, sometimes provided . . . by the real-life experiences of the audience."[18]

The strong link between reconciliation and forgiveness to anger and guilt becomes apparent when we realize that forgiveness is difficult for us because we are either angry/hurt by a transgression perpetrated against us by another or we feel guilt/shame because our transgressions caused someone else harm. Forgiveness then requires that we heal the memory of these events by "drain[ing] out our old fears and feelings and pour[ing] in Christ's feelings when we take his hand."[19] African-American storytelling provides a way to accomplish this task by equating memories to wounds. This idea gives a more vivid image of the damage done by wrongdoing and the process necessary to heal. "Forgiving [then]. . . is the art of healing inner wounds inflicted by. . . wrong[doings]."[20]

The recovery time from physical wounds varies with the severity of the wound. "Memories, like deep wounds, usually take weeks or even months to heal. . . . By healing memories every day, we will find ourselves not only moving from stage to stage but also penetrating each stage at a greater depth until we begin seeing the moment as God does."[21] At the root of our recovery time is four emotions. They are anxiety, fear, anger, and guilt. "These four emotions if buried lead to emotional instability but if worked through lead to health."[22] Dennis and Matthew Linn link these emotions to the stages of healing that are taken from Elisabeth Kubler-Ross's five stages of dying: denial, anger, bargaining, depression, and acceptance. In the denial stage a person doesn't admit any hurt. As the hurt continues the person enters the anger stage where others are blamed for the hurt. In the third stage, the person realizes they must forgive, but feels certain conditions must be met before they can. When those conditions fail, the person enters the fourth stage, depression, where guilt arises for letting the hurt happen in the first place. In the final stage, a person is able to embrace the newness that results from the hurt.[23] "For Kubler-Ross, the biggest difference between the anger stage and the depression stage is that in the anger stage most of the anger is focused outward, and in the depression stage most of the anger is focused inward."[24] "Healing of memories works through the anger and guilt until the fear and anxiety that crippled us begins in the acceptance stage to be a gift."[25]

Memory, Reconciliation, and Faith Formation

The following story[26] is an example of not only African-American storytelling but also the crippling effects of unhealed trauma and how healing memories facilitate a person's ability to tell their story. Roger is a young gay

man who had gotten lost in depression for several years. He was an outgo-
ing young adult, involved in his parish from elementary school through high
school. He was a dancer and an "A" student with the desire to go on to college and become a forensic specialist in the criminal justice system. As Roger
began to apply to colleges and discern his future more concretely, he met a
guy who seemed to be the perfect partner to his life's goals. As the two grew
closer, Roger began to question God's love for him and the Church's teachings on homosexuality. He found it difficult to love another man and maintain
his participation in the life of the Church, so he stopped participating. He
did, however, attempt to maintain a private prayer life, while going to other
churches (Protestant) that welcomed gay couples. Life, however, did not
prove to be the bliss Roger hoped for. The lure of the relationship pulled at
Roger in such a way that he not only dropped out of college after one semes-
ter, but he also stopped dancing and spending time with family and friends.
In time, he discovered that the person he loved did not love him enough to
be honest and truthful. After two years, Roger broke off the relationship and
returned home. Upon returning home his mother insisted that he return to
Church and "get himself together." But getting himself together proved to be
Roger's unraveling. In the process of trying to go back to school, get a job,
and return to Church, Roger was hindered by the memories of his past. Each
time he thought he'd take a step forward, he was reminded of his mistakes
and could not press on. He would often say that he had so much to make up
for and how could God forgive him anyway. Before long, Roger barely got
out of bed and if he did, he would end up on the couch watching TV or sitting
at his desk surfing the internet. It was difficult to get him to see life beyond his
past. This cycle continued for two years before Roger's mother finally asked
me to speak with him. It was during one of our conversations that I asked
Roger when he was going to forgive himself for what he had done. I went
on to say that much of his lethargy was due to his self-inflicted punishment
and inability to overcome the past. I then gave Roger permission to grieve
the past, to be angry about what happened and his role in it, and then to offer
himself forgiveness. When I said this, a light emanated from Roger showing
me that he was on his way from torment to joy.

Roger's story illustrates for us how the four core emotions mentioned earlier—anxiety, fear, anger, and guilt—hinder the healing of memory, thereby
hindering faith formation. "The key to dealing with the four core emotions
. . . is found in the twofold forgiveness of both the healing of memories and
the 'Our Father': forgive us (guilt), as we forgive those (anger)."[27] Healing
of memory then is connected to forgiveness, but not just forgiveness of
the other, the one outside self who has harmed us. This "forgiving is a gift
God has given us for healing ourselves before we are ready to help anyone
else[.]"[28]

The healing that must take place requires that we admit we are in conflict with ourselves and allow the "conflict [to open] a path, a holy path, toward revelation and reconciliation."[29] In opening a path, reconciliation can be seen as a journey. "As a journey, reconciliation is understood as both the flight away and the daring trip back. Ultimately, reconciliation is a journey toward and through conflict. . . . The journey through conflict toward reconciliation always involves turning to face oneself."[30] "Facing oneself and one's own fears and anxieties (trauma) demands an outward and inward journey. Along the journey of conflict, we always encounter ourselves, and in doing so, we come face to face with God, our Maker, whose image we bear, and who calls on us to "return.""[31]

In returning, we discover "[our] mission . . . to align ourselves with God, who is working to bring all things together, to reconcile all of creation and particularly a broken, estranged humanity."[32] This understanding is key to helping the People of God reconcile themselves. "When we are rooted in who we are, in who God has made us, we appreciate what we can do and actually celebrate our limitations. In addition, we accept that we have made mistakes and brought sin into our lives by our own bad choices."[33]

When Roger began to grieve his past, heal the memory (trauma), he realized he was "holding onto anger, hate and vengeance destroy[ing] any possibility of finding peace."[34] He found that by returning to the place of pain armed with forgiveness instead of denial, he was able to move past his anger and guilt, discovering that "forgiveness not only heals us; it sets us free."[35] A result of Roger's journey is that he has gone back to Church. Though he isn't active in the life of the Church, he is attending a small faith-sharing group where he is learning to enter into other "painful scene[s in his memory] with Christ and observe how He acts and speaks. Christ enters the memory not only to heal our sore spots with His words and touch, but also to heal those who have offended us."[36]

Healing of memories is necessary to assist us in faith formation since faith moves in and through memory, as recorded in scripture. "Faith requires commitment if it is to develop and grow."[37] Therefore, more work will have to be done, in the faith formation process that introduces us to a more committed relationship with God. It is through this relationship that we will "develop a better relationship with self and that love relationship allows for self-appreciation which leads [us] to be honest about self with self."[38] In handing on the faith, we must also let the People of God know that "forgiveness is at the very heart of the Christian message . . . [and] Christianity is not a religion of perfect people, but of forgiven people."[39]

This faith formation (catechesis) will be most effective when storytelling is utilized. "Stories are powerful means for shaping our identities. They weave together in a narrative the events that have special significance for us."[40] "Significant too about the best of our stories is that they can be recast as our contexts change and as we gain new insights into ourselves and our communities."[41] Though storytelling doesn't seem like a catechetical tool because it can conjure up notions of fiction, it is not foreign to the Catholic faith which sustains the oral tradition of the Scriptures, both Old and New Testament. Similar to retelling of scripture stories, intergenerational faith formation must also include the retelling of our stories. "What happens in the telling and retelling of the story is the healing of memory. . . . Once a new perspective is gained on a particularly traumatic experience, the story must be retold— and not only that story, but many other stories as well."[42]African-American storytelling provides a context in which the People of God can ground their experience of God to grow in faith.

In this chapter I spoke about intergenerational and historical trauma and the role memory plays in storytelling and how the inability to forgive and reconcile harmful memories prohibits the telling of one's story. In the next chapter I will offer intergenerational catechetical strategies and an evaluation of the My Story-Your Story Method.

NOTES

1. Genesis 3:7–24.
2. Matthew 26–27, Mark 15–15, Luke 22–23, John 18–19.
3. Dirk G. Lange, *Trauma Recalled: Liturgy, Disruption, and Theology* (Minneapolis, MN: Fortress Press, 2010), 6.
4. William S. Schmidt, "Theological and Spiritual Resources for Trauma," Unpublished Paper Dated February 12, 2018, and shared with the author during an in-person interview September 26, 2018. Schmidt is Professor of Pastoral Theology with an emphasis in Pastoral Counseling at the Institute of Pastoral Studies at Loyola University Chicago, 1.
5. Schmidt, 1.
6. U.S. Department of Health and Human Services Administration for Children and Families, https://www.acf.hhs.gov/trauma-toolkit/trauma-concept (accessed March 6, 2020).
7. Támara Hill, "Intergenerational Trauma in Families—8 Signs," *PsychCentral*, December 10, 2018, https://youtu.be/Nu5JC4iZdbw.YouTube *Channel, Támara Hill, MS NCC CCTP LPC* "8 Signs of Family Problems: Inter-generational Trauma— Psychotherapy Crash Course," November 13, 2018, https://www.youtube.com/w atch?v=6MU7all5364&t=376s and "Family Curse? Identifying Inter-generational Trauma," June 1, 2018, https://youtu.be/RCAPrlXqB-E (all accessed March 4, 2020).
8. Shelly Rambo, *Resurrecting Wounds: Living in the Afterlife of Trauma* (Waco, TX: Baylor University Press, 2017), 74.
9. Molly S. Castelloe, "How Trauma Is Carried Across Generations," *Psychology Today*, May 28, 2012, https://www.psychologytoday.com/us/blog/the-me-in-we/20 1205/how-trauma-is-carried-across-generations (accessed March 5, 2020).
10. Gates, Jr., 17–18.

11. Robert J. Schreiter, *The Ministry of Reconciliation: Spirituality and Strategies* (Maryknoll, NY: Orbis Press, 1998), 67.

12. Schreiter, 58.

13. Schreiter, 14.

14. Jones, 86.

15. Antoinette Bosco, *Radical Forgiveness* (Maryknoll, NY: Orbis Press, 2009), x.

16. Avis Clendenen and Troy Martin, *Forgiveness: Finding Freedom through Reconciliation* (NY: The Crossroad Publishing Company, 2002), 14.

17. Scheub, 13–14.

18. Scheub, 15.

19. Dennis Linn and Matthew Linn, *Healing Life's Hurts: Healing Memories through the Five Stages of Forgiveness* (New York/New Jersey: Paulist Press, 1974), 2.

20. Lewis B. Smedes, *The Art of Forgiving: When You Need to Forgive and Don't Know How* (Nashville, TN: Moorings, 1996), xii–xiii.

21. Linn and Linn, 17.

22. Linn and Linn, 24.

23. Linn and Linn, 11.

24. Linn and Linn, 12.

25. Linn and Linn, 25.

26. This fictional story is based on actual events.

27. Linn and Linn, 27.

28. Smedes, xii.

29. John Paul Lederach, *The Journey Toward Reconciliation*. Scottdale (Pennsylvania: Herald Press, 1999), 14.

30. Lederach, 23.

31. Lederach, 24.

32. Lederach, 160.

33. Brett C. Hoover, *Losing Your Religion, Finding Your Faith: Spirituality for Young Adults* (Mahweh, NJ:Paulist Press, 1998), 83.

34. Bosco, 35.

35. Lucy Fuchs, *Forgiveness: God's Gift of Love* (Staten Island: Alba House, 1990), 4.

36. Dennis Linn and Matthew Linn, *Healing of Memories: Prayer and Confession—Steps to Inner Healing* (New York/New Jersey: Paulist Press, 1974), 30.

37. Hoover, 23.

38. Dennis Linn and Matthew Linn, *Healing Life's Hurts*, 63.

39. Fuchs, 4.

40. Schreiter, 19.

41. Schreiter, 20.

42. Schreiter, 44–45.

Chapter 5

Intergenerational Catechetical Strategies

Words carry messages, both true and false, that shape our thinking which in turn affects our relationships. In the previous chapters, I have shown the cultural influences that have shaped the five generations alive today in the United States. I have introduced storytelling, in particular African-American storytelling, as a means to not only carry forth the Catholic faith but heal the wounds of trauma trapped in our memories. I have discussed the relationship between faith formation and catechesis, illustrating the importance of theological reflection in the process. As a catechetical method, I showed how African-American storytelling liberates us by helping us find the relevance of our own story in the Story of Jesus as revealed in scripture. "To know and use your voice you need to hear and read and interpret other voices, other stories. The act of voice counts on someone else listening and preparing to respond."[1]

As we mature, we understand our living in and through story. As Catholic Christians the narration of our story finds order and grounding in the Story of God who acts in and through our human living. However, this order is not always easily found amid the chaos of the world. African-American storytelling, with roots in chaos and uncertainty, provides a method of catechesis because it addresses the whole person, mind, body, spirit—the complex social and cultural realities that encompass people's lives—allowing for a more holistic understanding of the Catholic faith. Before offering strategies for intergenerational catechesis, I want to address the gifts or advantages to thinking about catechesis intergenerationally.

CONNECTING GENERATIONS

Stories help shape our culture and context in positive and negative ways.[2] When the voices of others are not present for whatever reason, we find ourselves telling stories that do not encompass all that is possible. Intergenerational storytelling stretches the imagination to include interpretations new and old to allow us to better prepare our communities for the kin-dom of God. "Now, more than ever, we need to be engaged in intergenerational dialogue as there are forces at play that are keeping generations from bridging gaps."[3] Herring reminds us that generations were more connected in the past, creating natural opportunities for conversations across the generations, but we have since moved away from this. He states,

> When previous generations arrived in this country it was the norm to have two, if not three, generations living under one roof. Today there are senior neighborhoods with age restrictions. . . . Or there are young, urban neighborhoods with trendy restaurants and coffee shops that do not have a gray hair around for miles. With living becoming more segregated by generation, we have become one step removed from having intergenerational engagement on a daily basis.[4]

He notes that older generations are in fact interested in engaging younger people, but they are unsure of how. "I still feel that I have something to offer those who are younger, but I can't find a way to connect with them. There aren't any places for me to naturally interact with people of different generations."[5] A shift in how we do catechesis can be the place where this connection happens. "These older individuals were not interested in creating a new initiative or leading a program. They . . . were eager to engage with younger individuals about contemporary issues, curious about how they were living life today, and interested in hearing about how they saw their future."[6] African-American storytelling can help move us away from Google for fact-checking into "the lived experiences, empathy, and inventiveness that someone older has acquired."[7] The framework of Herring's book will assist me in outlining intergenerational catechetical strategies. He calls this framework "three truths":[8]

1. We need fulfilling relationships with people our own age and across the generations to lead lives that are rich in meaning and purpose.
2. Social and technological revolutions create powerful waves of isolation that disconnect us from one another.
3. Regardless of age, we're all experiencing a feeling of ongoing disequilibrium, as if we can never adapt quickly enough to the changes swirling around us. Whether you're eighty or twenty-eight years old, if you

consider how you're living many aspects of your life today, they are probably different than only a few years ago and are likely to be different a few years from now.

So how do we go about creating intergenerational catechesis in a culture that continues to create separate spaces based on age? I offer three levels of strategies.[9] These levels are personal, parish, and diocesan. These strategies are intended for all persons who lead a ministry or seek to lead a ministry, including catechists where faith formation and spiritual growth are the focus. Stated this way, you can most definitely find yourself included. The first level of strategy, personal, cultivates story within each person including the catechist. This level asks us to pay attention to our own generation and the cultural influences that have shaped us—prompting us to look deeply at the things that have made an impact on our lives. The second and third levels of strategy illustrate concrete ways to engage in African-American storytelling for catechesis.

PERSONAL STRATEGIC LEVEL

My Story-Your Story calls our attention to the personal dimension of story. It seeks a level of intimacy and vulnerability that many may not be ready for, not only with regard to the other but most importantly with regard to one's self. African-American storytelling changes the way we approach catechesis in that the catechist's experience, tradition, and culture are as important as the topic presented. The catechist no longer disappears from the Story, but is part of it. By bringing one's own insight and transformed response to the Story, the catechist makes it possible for others to also see themselves in the Story, capable also of a transformed response.

The personal strategic level is necessary for all ministers and catechists who seek to use African-American storytelling as a method of catechesis because African-American storytelling includes the personal witness of the storyteller. A catechist intent on conveying a theme separate from her/his personal story decreases the possibility of transformation. A story will not carry the significance intended if the teller is not aware of the story's personal implications and personal impact. Therefore, to use African-American storytelling the storyteller must first become comfortable with her/his own story. This narrative journey consists of shaping my story, linking my story to the Story, and narrating my story.

Shaping My Story

Shaping my story is a process for the storyteller to become comfortable with her/his own story. This process involves a series of activities that include remembering, meditating, and theological reflection. It is important that the storyteller be aware of and bring to the activities that which makes her/him distinct: culture, tradition, and experience. These aspects help the storyteller engage the contemporary culture/context with her/his own culture/context in relation to experience and tradition. In other words, the storyteller's story finds its own life before being placed in dialogue with the Story. "Through the telling of our own stories, . . . we dare to explore the unfinished story we continue to create until we draw our last breath."[10] Shaping one's own story provides the personal witness necessary to use African-American storytelling, for story breathes life, one person to another. Dan McAdams tells us that our own narrative, which we begin to create in late adolescence and early adulthood is "complete with gods and goddesses, heroes and villains, tales of power and love, creation, demise, the rise, the fall, the rebirth, and adventures of the self."[11] The activities in shaping my story help bring to the forefront the tales we have created so that we can explore them and learn from them.

Though the activities may be done in a group, they are more effective when done alone. The time allotted for each activity depends on each person; it should not be rushed, nor should it take more than several weeks. The first activity is to create a timeline of significant (meaningful) events in one's life up to the present. The more events the better, because the events give body to the shaping of my story. Examples of significant/meaningful events are trips to summer camp, learning to cook, bullying and/or being bullied, graduation from elementary school, first job, getting a driver's license, divorce, leaving home for college, births/deaths, illness, Confirmation, job hiring/termination, First Communion, call to ministry, and retirement. The list could go on. It is important to know that what is significant/meaningful to one person may not be significant or meaningful to another. This is not a place of comparison, but a place of coming to know and understand. The duration of this activity can be shortened by listing only major events, however, doing so, does not allow for a full exploration of my story.

The second activity is to meditate on the events in the timeline, recalling any emotions, prejudices, attitudes, biases and reactions, personal or otherwise, associated with the events. A description of the emotions, prejudices, attitudes, biases, and reactions is added to the timeline next to each event so that the storyteller can begin the process of addressing these feelings that will resurface in the narration of the story. In this way, the storyteller is aware of them beforehand. It is here that the storyteller becomes more aware of outside influences like culture, context, and tradition. "The intent here is to discover our individual truth that will lead us to the 'Grandeur of God.' "[12] This activity may take several days, as the recall may bring to light things that need to be addressed with others before moving forward. Paula Sullivan reminds us to "not wrestle over the facts [of our story]; the intent is to discover the meaning of these events in our lives."[13] She goes on to say that "exploring personal history requires willingness and courage to be open to re-experiencing early events. Two conditions may interfere: fear of beginning such a task or . . . mulling over an event too long." It is for this reason that to fully enter into this activity one should do it alone. If done with a group, participants should be allowed to move into private space. Once this activity is complete, the storyteller is better prepared to assist others in shaping their story.

The third activity is to silently read through the timeline. The shape of the story begins to form through this reading, complete with the emotions, prejudices, attitudes, biases, and reactions associated with each event. The silent reading activity should be repeated several times before the storyteller ever reads the timeline aloud. The familiarity with one's own story before speaking it aloud increases the comfort level when it comes to telling it. As the story is read aloud, the storyteller becomes aware of the power of spoken words—her/his own spoken word. In order to read it aloud, add words that give a more complete description of each event and to aid in the movement from one event to the next. Here is an example of the three steps from my own timeline:

Significant event—Mother diagnosed with dementia

Meditating on my Mother's dementia—denial, anger, exposure, What will people think?, Why my Mom? Why me? life disruption, resignation, acceptance, grief, an opportunity to love unconditionally, service, uncertainty, fear

Silent reading to reading aloud—When I first discovered something was different about my Mom, I denied the possibility. After her official diagnosis of dementia, I was angry and felt exposed, wondering what would people think about me and her when we were in public. I was not eager for the disruption to my life often asking God, "Why my Mom? Why me?" Eventually, I accepted my Mom as she is now, grieving what was lost, but looking forward to the opportunities to love her unconditionally. There are still days where I am frightened and full of uncertainty facing the fact that I can no longer go to my Mother the way I used to.

The spoken words added to the timeline illustrate how story is formed from the facts of one's life. Once the storyteller has become comfortable with speaking her/his story, the process may be entered into again, starting with the first activity, adding more events that continue to shape the story. As the storyteller shapes her/his story, the Story looms larger.

Linking My Story to the Story

My story finds its fullness of meaning when linked to the Story by helping the storyteller move beyond the personal into the communal. To move beyond the personal, the storyteller puts into dialogue her/his experience, the story shaped, with the Christian tradition to see God acting in and through his/her life.[14] After identifying the action of God, the storyteller adds this to the timeline of events. The familiarity with my story is then enhanced as the storyteller sees the actions of God throughout the timeline. The linking of my story to the Story opens the storyteller to better understand her/his life as being in communion with God and others. At this point, the spoken words of my story take on new life as the storyteller is able to tell my story with God's Story. Going back to my example, I was able to move through my grief when I asked the questions "Why my Mom? Why me?" What I realized was that I was asking God these questions. I was wrestling like Jacob, before he went to meet Esau, trying to get a blessing from God that I was unsure I deserved or even needed. The more I struggled and asked questions, the more God was present, in my disappointment and my joy. In recounting history, culture, wisdom, knowledge, the storyteller grounds her/his experiences in God, who calls the storyteller to active participation in the kin-dom.

Narrating My Story

We tell stories that inform others of the ideas/situations/circumstances we are experiencing. In and through our story another person is affected, life is shared. The purpose then of sharing my story "is to discover the great mystery of becoming, the great mystery of God's presence in our lives."[15] The narration of my story moves beyond the storyteller into the "public": brief introductions at meetings; round-table discussions at conferences; faith expression at bible study; and social outreach involvement. The ingenuity of African-American storytelling is in the narration of my story which opens the pathway for your story to be shared. By doing so, the way in which catechesis is done should change. No longer lead by traditional themes that ensure knowledge of the Catholic faith as led by the *Catechism of the Catholic Church*, catechists who use African-American storytelling allow the themes to arise from the stories shared, which then lead back to the *Catechism*. The *My Story-Your Story* bond unites the storyteller and listener to work more efficiently in spreading the gospel, because of the relational aspect of story. The sections that follow outline parish and diocesan strategies for *My Story-Your Story*.

PARISH LEVEL STRATEGIES

In recent years, parish ministers found themselves seeking ways to involve young adults in parish life. They would invite young adults into the Church and encourage them to join a ministry only to discover a dead end; young adults didn't feel welcomed. With the onset of COVID-19 and stay-at-home directives, parish ministers must now reimagine parish activity and engagement for all generations. The wisdom of African-American storytelling as a method of catechesis in the parish is that it changes the parish into a welcoming one as it builds a network of persons who have narrated their story. In this section, I outline three strategies, two in-person and one virtual, for using African-American storytelling at the parish level.

Parishes are often wary about starting a new program, especially one that that doesn't have a proven track record. African-American storytelling as a method of catechesis is not a new program for the parish, but a method that may enhance current catechetical endeavors. It is a way of drawing upon the experiences of all persons and celebrating them in communion. African-American storytelling does, however, require the personal involvement, as described in the previous section, of all persons involved in ongoing faith formation: the pastor, catechists, and parish ministers. African-American storytelling allows these ministers to connect their life experience to their beliefs, validating their living, becoming a welcoming parish.

Strategy for Catechists

Current catechetical methods need to be challenged in how they foster faith formation and spiritual enrichment. The "banking" method of teaching, depositing information into people's minds for withdrawal later, has left too many of us with a bankrupt knowledge of the Catholic faith.[16] Left with insufficient faith information, many move on to a faith they can understand or simply rely on being "spiritual, not religious." Faith understood within the context of day-to-day living is important for all of us, especially in the context of the social isolation that is called for to contain the spread of COVID-19. The African-American storytelling method of catechesis, with its focus on experience and orality, moves away from the "banking" method toward a dialogical one, *My Story-Your Story*, where solutions offer better ways to deal with this world.

Following is a guideline for catechists who have already completed the personal strategic level activities mentioned above.

Setting the Schedule and Environment

Schedule the sessions on a weekday evening at least twice a month, such as, first and third Mondays for two hours. The frequency is important so that people are not overwhelmed by meeting too many times or underserved by not meeting often enough. The balance of twice a month takes into account absences. For example, if someone cannot attend a session, a once a month meeting means that she/he must wait an entire month before another gathering takes place. The duration of the session is important to be seen as a manageable amount of time. Once the days and times are set, keep them. Most of us prefer knowing that our faith formation sessions are "permanent." The space should lend itself to intimacy, where people can engage in dialogue without raising their voices to be heard and persons walking by cannot hear the conversation. This space can be in the church, the rectory, a restaurant with a private dining area, or even someone's home. Tables and chairs should be set up so that everyone is sitting around the table facing one another, individuals in a group. Care should be taken to use the same space for each meeting as doing so creates a stable environment and allows participants to attend when they can, knowing the location and time are the same. Place objects in the space that call one's attention to the Catholic faith, such as, a cross/crucifix, a rosary, decorative cloth, a bible, a candle, and carafe with water. These sacramentals should be present at every meeting. Hospitality (food and beverages) should be included within the space, not in a separate area. This allows participants to move freely about the space without missing parts of the conversation.

The Invitation

The invitation should include the type of session being held and the benefit of attending. It is important to be clear on the intent of the sessions, whether they are bible study, spiritual enrichment, or faith formation sessions. People interested in bible study need to know that these sessions will focus on faith-sharing. For the purposes of this discussion, our sessions will be faith forma-tion sessions.

   In good church fashion, put the information about the sessions in the bul-letin, post it on the parish website, make an announcement from the pulpit, but mostly rely on personal invitation. Personal invitation extends the hand of Jesus and conveys the message that you notice the person, she/he is impor-tant. Personal invitation also allows you to speak more about the sessions and explain why the person should come. African-American storytelling can play a part even here as your invitation may include a bit of my story, for example,

> Hi Carol. How are you? I'm starting a small faith formation group here at the parish and I'd like you to be a part of it. Yes I know you're busy, but it would really mean a lot to me if you came. The more I hear about the struggles young adults have with the faith, the more determined I am to help. I don't want young adults to struggle like I did because of lack of knowledge and understanding. It was good seeing you. I hope you can join the group. It meets two weeks from Monday at 7pm in the Venerable Augustus Tolton Room.

This dialogue changes to match each person and the generation they belong to, for example, "Hi Mr. Frank. How are things going? I'm starting a small faith formation group here at the parish and I'd like you to be a part of it. Your wisdom and experience would be an anchor for the group. Far too few of us know or understand the struggles of World War II veterans. Our first meeting is Monday at 7pm in the Venerable Augustus Tolton Room."

Invitations cannot be onetime occurrences. They must be extended until the person comes to a session and then may have to be extended again should they stop coming. Invitation is not only about "recruiting" people to attend the sessions, but it's also about listening. This requires the invitation to be part of a conversation. When inviting youth and teens, make sure that the invitation includes their parents—we don't want any misunderstandings. What you want to convey in all your invitations is "All—ages, genders, sexual orientation—are welcome."

The Session

Greetings are important in shaping the session, therefore welcome/greet each person who arrives with a handshake, hug, or other appropriate gesture. Acknowledge late arrivals, with a brief recap of what has taken place. Greet them personally at a break. Briefly introduce yourself and invite others to do the same. Introductions at this point need not be more than one's name. There will be time later for people to speak more about themselves. If there are no new people, introductions are not necessary. Open each gathering with prayer, noting that the time allotted for prayer should fit into the two-hour window. Feel free to introduce different prayer styles as the group continues to meet, including explanations of the prayer styles in the evening's discussion. After prayer introduce the topic and break for hospitality.

Expounding upon the topic begins after the break. It is important to note that all generations involved should be present, not to be separated into age groups. Using the African-American storytelling method of *My Story-Your Story*, the topic comes to life through the sharing of all the generations present. The African-American storytelling method teaches, encourages, and challenges. No matter one's style of teaching, whether it is to lecture and/ or use multimedia, as the storyteller, my story needs to be part of the lesson. Including my story in the lesson illustrates your knowledge of the topic through experience, whether positive or negative. The emphasis is on experience. Here you may see clearer why the personal response activities should be done before using this method with others.

The African-American storytelling method not only requires you to tell story, but it also requires you to listen to story. After sharing my story through the lesson, invite the participants to share your story. Ask questions to help them get started, that is, "What difference does prayer make in your life? What happened when you prayed for something and got it/didn't get it?" Be aware that not everyone will share your story and they should not be pressured to do so. In time each person will come to share. The *My Story-Your Story* connections help move the discussion to theological reflection where participants gain clarity on God's actions in and through the stories shared. This leads to the Story.

Having heard the stories of those present, you now reecho the part of the Story that is relevant to the chosen topic. In the previous paragraph, prayer was used as an example. Staying with prayer as a topic, this is the Story—the prayers of the Catholic Church: history, usage, devotions—that you would be sharing. Participants are now challenged to see the connection between their story and the Story, thereby gaining more insight into their own story. This awareness draws them toward a response and/or action which you encourage by asking questions like: "What does prayer call you to do or be? In what way do you see prayer shaping the community?" This part of the session may be challenging for some since it calls each person to accountability, first to their story then to how their story affects another's story. "By sharing our stories and listening to another's, we transcend the boundaries of self and move toward understanding the timelessness of God's life in all human beings."[17] The session ends with prayer after general announcements and the topic for the next gathering.

This strategy asks that the role of catechists be re-envisioned from merely reechoing the Story from texts and age-based curriculums, to reechoing the Story through *My Story-Your Story*. This change in faith formation allows for each person's culture/context, traditions and experience to be part of the process. When these aspects are part of the lessons, a transformed response results in conversion that better understands the formation of God's kin-dom. This strategy also shows how catechists can use African-American storytelling as a method for catechesis without starting a new program. When African-American storytelling is also used by the pastoral ministers/staff this strategy is reinforced.

Strategy for Pastoral Ministers/Staff

In this time of social distancing and social isolation many people are seeking guidance, especially spiritually. "Social isolation is a significant societal issue and fostering organic relationships across generations is one way that people of all ages can ease their feelings of loneliness."[18] Many of us want someone to journey with us to help us realize that life doesn't have to be lived without God. Mentoring is a great way to do that and African-American storytelling as a method of catechesis can assist pastoral ministers/staff in giving witness to the faith. It is here that intergenerational "conversations potentially enable us to understand that each generation has a stake in the other's well-being."[19]As was the case with catechists, pastoral ministers/staff are to complete the personal strategic level before using this strategy.

As people build relationships through *My Story-Your Story*, they develop a greater sense of God, self, and other. Pastoral ministers/staff play a significant role in that they, along with catechists, are called to invite, welcome, and hand on the faith. Pastoral care that reflects the interests and concerns of the entire parish works in harmony with catechesis that validates each person and her/his experience. I propose a strategy for clergy and one for lay ministers/staff.

Clergy

In order to preach a relevant message it is important to listen to the needs and concerns of one's parishioners. There "is the need for greater conversation and advanced preparation for lives transitioning across the generational spectrum. That includes young adults experiencing a tumultuous time because of economic difficulties or elderly adults clinging to independence, unwilling to accept that they are putting themselves and others at risk."[20] *My Story-Your Story* helps in that it allows space for the conversations to take place. African-American storytelling then aids in your preaching as it requires you to engage the selected scripture text in a personal way. Sharing your personal journey with the text in the homily is what helps to make the preaching relevant. Include in your homily how you came up with the title. Share what the passage meant to you as a child and how the meaning changed as you matured. Though not all scripture passages will call forth a positive response from you, it is important to share that with the community. For example: Preaching about your struggle and dependence on God to "make a way out of no way" teaches and encourages those who often feel alone in the struggle.

On a weekly basis you have the opportunity to share the Story and my story, inviting your story. The People of God are listening when you send out this invitation and will respond. Help create an atmosphere that is intentionally welcoming. When you listen to people's stories use what you can in a homily. Such an action lets people know that you are paying attention to them. Remember, a current story is better than the one that has been forwarded through e-mail.

Lay Ministers/Staff

Having completed the personal strategic level, lay ministers and staff are challenged to point out ways in which African-American storytelling may take place in their current context. It is important to note that ministerial roles are catechetical in that they function to lead people to Christ or help strengthen people in Christ. African-American storytelling helps lay ministers and staff witness their Catholic faith as they share their "walk of faith." This witness in and through story may occur when the pastoral council meets to discuss the state of the parish, when the fundraising committee meets, and when ushers/ greeters gather. The opportunities to share one's faith journey are endless. "At its most basic level, the pool for participation in the community is what summons a group of people to meet regularly and primarily in person (that is, face-to-face) around a shared purpose for which they reciprocally care."[21] As lay ministers and staff make room for story, they further assist the People of God by serving as one-to-one mentors who share their my stories. Mentoring nurtures both parties while being intentional in word and deed.

Virtual Strategy

COVID-19 has many ministers scrambling to serve the People of God virtually. Though this strategy is a response for online ministry using African-American storytelling, it is limiting in that it only applies to those who have video and audio capability via a smartphone, tablet, or computer. "When people [are] in face-to-face communities, they [have] a better understanding of the impact that their words and actions . . . have on others. Often, they come to understand that they [are] accountable for what they [say], and [realize] how a word spoken directly to someone's face [can] change a life for the better or for the worse."[22] Encourage everyone to stay on camera for the duration of the session to promote community. The video-conferencing platform that is used is not the key factor here. What is important is that the group is small enough to allow for storytelling. I recommend that a virtual group not be larger than ten people including the facilitator (catechist, pastoral minister/ staff). The time allotted for the session should be limited to fifty to sixty minutes. This timeframe accounts for possible screen fatigue. Encourage people to come with their snacks and beverages so that they do not have to get up a too many times during the session.

The Virtual Session

Greetings are still important here. Welcome everyone to the "space," even those who arrive late, going over technical protocols like keeping microphones muted when not speaking. Open with a prayer, song, lectio/visio divina, meditation and/or silence. Whatever opening method used, ensure it is connected to the topic to be discussed. After the opening is complete allow a few minutes for general check-in, asking questions like, "How has the transition to meeting online impacted you?" The topic is now introduced and the catechist/pastoral minister expounds on the topic through my story. This is very much like the catechist session mentioned above. The main difference is the length of the story-sharing. The catechist/pastoral minister is no longer facilitating a two-hour session, so she/he needs to keep my story short to allow enough time for participants to share your story.

The online session can be challenging as people struggle with technology and looking at others' video images. The key is to keep the stories going by inviting each person to reflect on the topic through her/his experience, culture/context, and tradition. "When we share life events with another, the listener is also reminded of her story."[23] As the session comes to an end, thank everyone for coming and sharing and end with a prayer, song, lectio/ visio divina, meditation, or silence—possibly the same one you used to begin the session.

DIOCESAN STRATEGIC LEVEL

As people seek to make meaning of their existence, there is a growing demand for faith formation and catechesis. African-American storytelling as a method of catechesis offers diocesan offices a way to address people's catechetical concerns, revitalizing their faith. Departmental issues such as who will conduct the training or what department/agency does this fall under will not be addressed in this strategy since each diocesan structure varies. As a catechetical method, this strategy may be implemented by those responsible for faith formation and catechesis across age groups.

In the Personal Strategic Level section, I stated that all persons using African-American storytelling as a method of catechesis complete this process alone though it could be done in a group setting. In this section I address how to do this process for a group, in the form of a retreat entitled, "An Introduction to Using African-American Storytelling in Faith Formation." This retreat is for anyone interested in using African-American storytelling as a method of catechesis at the parish level. It is open to current African-American storytelling practitioners and those who wish to begin. This retreat seeks to introduce the African-American storytelling method of *My Story-Your Story* and engage participants in its performance.

An Introduction to Using African-American Storytelling in Faith Formation

The Retreat Content

This retreat takes place over the course of three full days, including time for personal prayer and reflection. There are nine sessions and two storytelling presentations. Each session will use African-American storytelling as the method of engaging the participants in the process. Session one covers the history and practice of African-American storytelling. Session two covers African-American storytelling and its relationship to faith and scripture. Session three introduces theological reflection and its role in prayer, our daily lives and this method. Session four is an actual theological reflection session.

Session five explains the connection of *My Story-Your Story*, while session six explores the freedom gained through story. Session seven begins the personal story familiarity process with shaping my story activities. Session eight continues the personal story familiarity with the linking my story to the Story activity. Session nine concludes the personal story familiarity with narrating my story. At the end of the retreat, participants are encouraged to return to their personal story on their own time to continue the process.

As a diocesan strategy, this retreat has the potential to enhance parish liturgies, reduce conflict between generations, and more effectively help multicultural parishes unite. Table 5.1 shows the flow of the retreat.

Table 5.1   The Retreat Schedule

	Day One	Day Two	Day Three
0800-0830	Arrival/Check-in	Breakfast	Breakfast
0845	Welcome/Retreat Facility Orientation		
0900	Prayer	Prayer	Prayer
0915-1015	Session 1—African-American Storytelling	Session 5—*My Story-Your Story*	Session 8—Linking My Story to the Story Activity
1030-1130	Session 2—African-American Storytelling, Faith and Scripture	Session 6—Freedom Through Story	Session 8 continues
1130-1215	Lunch	Lunch	Lunch
1230-1330	Personal Time	Personal Time	Session 9—Narrating My Story Activity
1345-1445	Session 3—Theological Reflection	Session 7—Shaping My Story Activities	Session 9 continues
1500-1645	Session 4—Theological Reflection Activity	Session 7 continues	Conclusion Closing Prayer
1700-1800	Dinner	Dinner	Dinner (optional)
1830-2000	Storytelling Presentation	Storytelling Presentation	
2030	Evening Prayer	Evening Prayer	

EVALUATING THE METHOD

I realize that measuring faith formation and spiritual development can only be done by the individual and challenged by the catechist. Yet I contend that the catechist is able to determine a person's starting point and measure progress through the dialogue that occurs. The fact that catechesis is ongoing and cyclical means that there will be setbacks as people face adversity. However personal, it is possible to measure the efficacy of African-American storytelling as a method of catechesis.

The evaluation consists of a series of surveys to be taken prior to using African-American storytelling, after using the method for three months or twelve weeks, and after one year. The survey is designed to gather current spiritual, liturgical, and service-oriented activity. This survey should be informal so all age groups can participate. It is not necessary for the survey to be written for distribution, but the responses of each person will need to be recorded for tracking purposes. You may suggest that those who are able, write out their responses so that they may see their own progress. The questions[24] for the survey are as follows:

- Is prayer a part of your life? If so, describe. If not, explain.
- Are you involved in any volunteer service-oriented activities such as feeding the hungry, working at a shelter, tutoring, coaching, or cleaning graffiti off buildings?
- Do you attend church services? If so, where and how often? If not, explain.
- For those of you who attend church services, do you participate in any ministry, organization, project at the church?

After using this method for three months/twelve weeks, the following should occur: increased frequency of personal prayer, participation in devotions and/or spiritual reading, increased church attendance or dialogue about attending church, participation in a volunteer service-oriented project. After one year, the following should occur: increased involvement in church ministry; facilitation of at least one weekly session. After two years of using this method, group facilitators should emerge and they should be able to facilitate the weekly sessions and/or start other groups; take on leadership roles in the church. It should be noted that the evaluation is not measuring a person's faith level, but the effectiveness of a method to "hand down" the faith.

INTERGENERATIONAL CATECHESIS

What makes the above strategies of catechesis intergenerational? To answer this question, I go back to Herring's framework of three truths mentioned earlier in this chapter. Herring's first truth encourages us to have relationships "with people our own age and across the generations to lead lives that are rich in meaning and purpose." African-American storytelling, rooted in the community—the family—the generations, is the framework to "sharing our stories [with] persons who are willing to listen without judgement."[25] The *My Story-Your Story* method of African-American storytelling shows us that other stories are needed for us to develop deeper meaning and purpose in life. When those stories stretch across the generations, we discover old stories that have wrestled with the Story and new stories just encountering the Story. Together, all our stories, old and new, help us better understand the Catholic faith and its intricacies, inviting us to become more active in our faith formation. The more active we are in our faith formation, the more our decision-making will be grounded in the good of the entire community.

Leaning heavily on African-American storytelling, *My Story-Your Story* captures the joys and sorrows of community, connects them to the good news—God's kin-dom is here and to come—and sets out pathways of faith-filled living and doing. Based on an understanding of family, intergenerational catechesis moves away from the domestic church as a starting point for growing in faith to the community as a starting point. This shift takes in the reality of family systems. The domestic church focuses on those who live in the household. Intergenerational catechesis focuses on everyone in the church community: single persons, divorced persons, widows/widowers, teens, young adults, pre-school and elementary children, parents, grandparents, aunts, and uncles.

NOTES

1. Callahan, 20.
2. The Connecting Generations subheading is taken from Hayim Herring's *Connecting Generations: Bridging the Boomer, Gen X, and Millennial Divide*(Lanham, MD: Rowman& Littlefield, 2019).
3. Herring, x.
4. Herring, xi.
5. Herring, xix.
6. Herring, xix.
7. Herring, xxi.
8. Herring, xxii.
9. These strategies were first published as pastoral responses. See Timone Davis, "My Story-Your Story: A Pastoral Response for 21st Century Catechesis," *The Journal of the Black Catholic Theological Symposium* 11 (2018): 79–95.
10. Paula Farrell Sullivan, *The Mystery of My Story: Autobiographical Writing for Personal and Spiritual Development* (Mahwah, NJ: Paulist Press, 1991), 5.

11. Dan P. McAdams, *Power, Intimacy, and the Life Story: Personological Inquiries into Identity* (New York: The Guilford Press, 1988), ix.

12. Sullivan, 7.

13. Sullivan, 10.

14. See theological reflection section in chapter three.

15. Sullivan, 7.

16. See Paulo Freire, *Pedagogy of the Oppressed*, 30th anniversary ed. (New York: Continuum, 2000), 72–81, where he discusses the banking concept of education.

17. Sullivan, 83.

18. Herring, 18.

19. Herring, 42.

20. Herring, 55.

21. Herring, 64.

22. Herring, 65.

23. Sullivan, 98.

24. These questions are not in any order of importance and may be modified to better accommodate your culture and context.

25. Sullivan, 99.

Conclusion

African-American storytelling "talks the talk" and "walks the walk" as a catechetical method to revive faith.

> Since the beginning of time folks have always wanted to spread the word. The ones who can spread the word the most effectively have the ability to "talk dat talk" and "walk dat walk." . . . In the African-American culture, past and present, these folks have gone by many names. Today they are called preachers, healers, teachers, comedians, blues singers, poets, dancers, rappers, liars, painters, and historians. . . . The storyteller, the story, and the audience are of equal importance.[1]

The equality of storyteller, story, and audience speaks to the bond of *My Story-Your Story* and the Story that I speak about in this book. I've tried to convey the importance of African-American storytelling for the U.S. Catholic Church by addressing the origin of African-American storytelling and its use in faith formation.

I began by exploring the current generations alive and the impact the U.S. culture has had on each of them. I noted that technology has shaped all generations, particularly Millennials. The nature of storytelling to evangelize was explored as I expanded the understanding of *My Story-Your Story*. "The goal . . . is to use storytelling to strengthen people's personal and interpersonal growth so that they can respond to God's salvation drama as it unfolds and as it has an impact on their lives."[2] The exploration of theological reflection helped me show how God's story intersects our lives, calling us to action. I spoke about intergenerational and historical trauma and memory highlighting the need for healing through forgiveness and reconciliation. I touched on the

liberating effects of storytelling before concluding with catechetical strategies for implementation.

My Story-Your Story contains some essential characteristics which I think
allow it to be used for the building up of the whole person. They are holistic,
transformative, and communal. We can no longer just hand over information
and expect people to accept it without addressing physical conditions, emotional well-being, and intellectual capabilities. African-American storytelling
as a method of catechesis opens the door for these concerns to be addressed
by listening and offering encouragement.

With so many things competing for our attention, the Church must compete in such a way as to not be filtered out. The Church has to embrace many
of the marketing strategies used in the business sector, for example, interac-
tive websites, social networking, video-sharing, and podcasting. This has
been proven by the current mandates of social distancing and the move to
online platforms for various social interactions. Pastors and their staff must
listen to the concerns of all generations and respond with respect and appreciation. Key to all the work that must be done in the Church today is mentoring. Although answering questions like "What is my purpose in life? What
is God's plan for me?" are not new questions for any generation, Millennial
and Generation Z Catholics are faced with more interference than any other
generation in attempting to respond. Therefore, mentoring provides the guidance necessary in a manner that is respectful and mutually beneficial. Hayim
Herring explains it this way:

> Young adults want to be heard and respected by those who are older. "Being
> heard" doesn't just mean people politely listening and agreeing during a con-
> versation. Rather, it means that the listener is curious and open to learning
> about another point of view. "Being respected" doesn't mean that someone else
> will automatically agree with your opinion on a given issue. In fact, they may
> challenge you. But it does mean that someone views you as capable of making
> thoughtful choices—even if it means making a mistake or two along the way.[3]

> Older people may feel like those around them no longer take them seriously,
> either because they're perceived as not being "productive," "tech savvy," or
> "aware of today's new realities." It's as if they've been stamped with a product
> expiration date that has passed.[4]

In my own work with young adults, I've helped them to discover that it
takes work to grow in faith and the transformation cannot be made from
the outside looking in. As they learn more about their faith, they find their
voice—a voice that demands silence sometimes in order to converse with
God and a voice not afraid to speak up in a room full of older Catholics.

Working with young adults is not always easy, given the many distractions with which they function. Yet, the fact that the Millennial and Generation Z Catholics are trying to navigate through the flood of information toward God's clarifying voice is hopeful.

NOTES

1. Goss and Barnes, 10.
2. Wimberly, *African American Pastoral Care*, 7.
3. Herring, 112.
4. Herring, 113.

Bibliography

Abrahams, Roger D. *African American Folktales: Stories from Black Traditions in the New World.* New York: Pantheon Books, 1985.

———. *African Folktales: Traditional Stories of the Black World.* New York: Pantheon Books, 1983.

Andrews, Dale P. *Practical Theology for Black Churches: Bridging Black Theology and African American Folk Religion.* Louisville: Westminster John Knox Press, 2002.

Bauman, Richard. *Story, Performance and Event.* Cambridge, England: Cambridge University Press, 1986.

Beaudoin, Tom. *Virtual Faith: The Irreverent Spiritual Quest of Generation X.* San Francisco, CA: Jossey-Bass, 1998.

Bevans, Stephen B. *Models of Contextual Theology: Faith and Cultures.* Rev. ed. Maryknoll, NY: Orbis Books, 2002.

Bosco, Antoinette. *Radical Forgiveness.* Maryknoll, NY: Orbis Books, 2009.

Butler, Jr. Lee H. *Liberating Our Dignity, Saving Our Souls.* St. Louis: Chalice Press, 2006.

Callahan, John F. *In the African-American Grain: Call and Response in Twentieth-Century Black Fiction.* Champaign, IL: University of Illinois Press, 2001.

Carter-Black, Jan. "Teaching Cultural Competence: An Innovative Strategy Grounded in the Universality of Storytelling as Depicted in African and African American Storytelling Traditions." *Journal of Social Work Education* 43, no. 1 (2007): 31–50.

Castelloe, Molly S. "How Trauma Is Carried Across Generations." *Psychology Today,* May 28, 2012. Accessed March 5, 2020. https://www.psychologytoday.com/us/blog/the-me-in-we/201205/how-trauma-is-carried-across-generations.

Champion, Tempii B. *Understanding Storytelling Among African American Children: A Journey From Africa to America.* Mahwah, NJ: Lawrence Erlbaum Associates, Publishers, 2003.

Clendenen, Avis and Troy Martin. *Forgiveness: Finding Freedom Through Reconciliation.* New York: The Crossroad Publishing Company, 2002.

Codrington, Raymond. "In the Beginning: Hip-Hop's Early Influences." Oxford African American Studies Center. Accessed March 2, 2020. http://www.oxfordaas c.com/public/features/archive/0806/essay.jsp.

Congregation for the Clergy. *General Directory for Catechesis*. Washington, DC: United States Catholic Conference, 1997.

Copeland, M. Shawn. "Method in Emerging Black Catholic Theology." In *Taking Down Our Harps: Black Catholics in the United States*, eds. Diana L. Hayes and Cyprian Davis. Maryknoll, NY: Orbis Books, 1998.

D'Antonio, William, James D. Davidson, Dean R. Hoge and Mary L Gautier. *American Catholics Today: New Realities of Their Faith and Their Church*. Lanham: Rowman and Littlefield Publishers, Inc., 2007.

Davis, Timone. "Cultural Colonization and Young Adult Liturgical Experience."*The Journal of the Black Catholic Theological Symposium* 12(2019): 87–104.

———. "My Story-Your Story: A Pastoral Response for 21st Century Catechesis." *The Journal of the Black Catholic Theological Symposium* 11 (2018): 79–95.

Dimock, Michael. "Defining Generations: Where Millennials End and Generation Z Begins." *Pew Research Center*, January 17, 2019. Accessed February 29, 2020. www.pewresearch.org/fact-tank/2019/01/17/where-millennials-end-and-generati on-z-begins/.

Dooley, Catherine. "Evangelization and Catechesis: Partners for a New Millennium." In *The Echo Within: Emerging Issues in Religious Education*, eds. Catherine Dooley and Mary Collins, 145–160. Allen, TX: Thomas More, 1997.

Eugene, Toinette. "Christian Education: A Ministry of the Word." In *Tell It Like It Is: A Black Catholic Perspective on Christian Education*, ed. Eva Marie Lumas, 3–17. Oakland: National Black Sisters' Conference, 1983.

Fonte, John. "E Pluribus Unum: The Bradley Project on America's National Identity." *The Bradley Project*, June 1, 2008. Accessed March 14, 2020.https://ww w.hudson.org/research/14149-e-pluribus-unum-the-bradley-project-on-america-s -national-identity.

Francis. *Christ is Alive! Christus Vivit: Post-synodal Apostolic Exhortation*. Washington, DC: United States Conference of Catholic Bishops, 2019.

Freire, Paulo. *Pedagogy of the Oppressed*. 30th Anniversary ed. New York: Continuum, 2000.

Fuchs, Lucy. *Forgiveness: God's Gift of Love*. Staten Island: Alba House, 1990.

Gallagher, Michael Paul. *Clashing Symbols: An Introduction to Faith and Culture*. NewYork/Mahwah, NJ: Paulist Press, 2003.

Gates, Jr., Henry Louis. "Introduction: Narration and Cultural Memory in the African-American Tradition." In *Talk That Talk: An Anthology of African-American Storytelling*, eds. Linda Goss and Marian E. Barnes, 15–19. New York: Simon and Schuster, 1989.

Gaylor, Dennis. "Generational Differences." *U.S. Fish and Wildlife*. Accessed May 6, 2020. https://training.fws.gov/supervisors/update/episode2/documents/generat ionaldifferenceschart.pdf.

Google. Accessed February 29, 2020. https://www.sites.google.com/site/btcsit/gene rations-of-computers.

Goss, Linda and Marian E. Barnes, eds. *Talk That Talk: An Anthology of African-American Storytelling*. New York: Simon and Schuster, 1989.

Groome, Thomas H. *Christian Religious Education: Sharing Our Story and Vision*. San Francisco: Harper and Row, 1981. Reprint, San Francisco: Jossey-Bass, 1999.

Groome, Thomas H. and Harold Daly Horell, eds. *Horizons and Hopes: The Future of Religious Education*. New York/Mahwah, NJ: Paulist Press, 2003.

Harris, James Henry. *The Word Made Plain: The Power and Promise of Preaching*. Minneapolis: Fortress Press, 2004.

Hater, Robert J. *Tell Me A Story: The Role of Narrative in the Faith Life of Catholics*. New London, CT: Twenty Third Publications, 2006.

———. *The Relationship Between Evangelization and Catechesis*. Washington, DC: National Conference of Diocesan Directors of Religious Education, 1981.

Hayes, Diana L. *And Still We Rise: An Introduction to Black Liberation Theology*. New York/Mahwah, NJ: Paulist Press, 1996.

Hayes, Diana L. and Cyprian Davis, O.S.B. eds. *Taking Down Our Harps: Black Catholics in the United States*. Maryknoll: Orbis Books, 1998.

Hayes, Mike. *Googling God: The Religious Landscape of People in their 20s and 30s*. New York/Mahwah, NJ: Paulist Press, 2007.

Herring, Hayim. *Connecting Generations: Bridging the Boomer, Gen X, and Millennial Divide*. Lanham, MD: Rowman & Littlefield, 2019.

Hess, Mary E. "Finding a Way into Empathy through Story Exercises in a Religious Studies Classroom." *Religious Studies News*. Accessed October 19, 2020. https://rsn.aarweb.org/spotlight-on/teaching/empathy/story-exercises-religious-studies-classroom.

Hill, Kenneth H. *Religious Education in the African American Tradition: A Comprehensive Introduction*. St. Louis: Chalice Press, 2007.

Hill, Támara. "Intergenerational Trauma in Families—8 Signs." *Psych Central*. https://youtu.be/Nu5JC4iZdbw. *YouTube Channel, Támara Hill, MS NCC CCTP LPC*. Accessed March 4, 2020. https://www.youtube.com/watch?v=6MU7all5364&t=376s and https://youtu.be/RCAPrlXqB-E.

Hoge, Dean R., William D. Dinges, Mary Johnson, and Juan L. Gonzales, Jr. *Young Adult Catholics: Religion in the Culture of Choice*. Notre Dame, IN: University of Notre Dame Press, 2001.

Hoover, Brett C. *Losing Your Religion Finding Your Faith: Spirituality for Young Adults*. New York/Mahwah, NJ: Paulist Press, 1998.

Hughes, Kathleen. *Saying Amen: A Mystagogy of Sacrament*. Chicago: Liturgy Training Publications, 1999.

Jones, Gayl. *Liberating Voices: Oral Tradition in African American Literature*. Harvard University Press, 1991.

Jones, Nathan. *Sharing the Old, Old Story: Educational Ministry in the Black Community*. Winona, MN: St. Mary's Press, 1982.

Kouyate, D'Jimo. "The Role of the Griot." In *Talk That Talk: An Anthology of African-American Storytelling*, eds. Linda Goss and Marian E. Barnes, 179–181. New York: Simon and Schuster, 1989.

Kyllonen, Tommy. *Un.orthodox: Church, Hip-Hop, Culture*. Grand Rapids, MI: Zondervan, 2007.

Lange, Dirk G. *Trauma Recalled: Liturgy, Disruption, and Theology.* Minneapolis, MN: Fortress Press, 2010.

Lartey, Emmanuel. "Practical Theology as Theological Form." In *The Blackwell Reader in Pastoral and Practical Theology*, eds. James Woodward and Stephen Pattison, 129–134. Malden, MA: Blackwell, 2000.

Lederach, John Paul. *The Journey Toward Reconciliation.* Scottdale, PA: Herald Press, 1999.

Linn, Dennis and Matthew Linn. *Healing Life's Hurts: Healing Memories Through the Five Stages of Forgiveness.* New York/New Jersey: Paulist Press, 1978.

———. *Healing of Memories: Prayer and Confession—Steps to Inner Healing.* New York/New Jersey: Paulist Press, 1974.

Marquardt, Elizabeth. *Between Two Worlds: The Inner Lives of Children of Divorce.* New York: Crown Publishers, 2005.

McAdams, Dan P. *Power, Intimacy, and the Life Story: Personological Inquiries into Identity.* New York: The Guilford Press, 1988.

McKenna, Megan and Tony Cowan. *Keepers of the Story.* Maryknoll, NY: Orbis Press, 1997.

Merriam-Webster. Accessed March 4, 2020. http://www.merriamwebster.com/dictionary/latchkey+child?show=0&t=1300736489; http://www.merriam-webster.com/dictionary/middle%20class; http://www.merriam-webster.com/dictionary/testimony.

Miller, Craig Kennet and MaryJane Pierce Norton. *Making God Real for a New Generation: Ministry with Millennials Born from 1982 to 1999.* Nashville: Discipleship Resources, 2003.

Miller, Vincent J. *Consuming Religion: Christian Faith and Practice in a ConsumerCulture.* New York: Continuum, 2005.

Mitchell, Ella. "Black Nurture." In *Black Church Lifestyles: Rediscovering the Black Christian Experience*, compiler Emmanuel L. McCall, 45–67. Nashville: Broadman Press, 1986.

Mitchell, Henry H. "Black Preaching." In *Black Church Lifestyles: Rediscovering the Black Christian Experience*, compiler Emmanuel L. McCall, 105–126. Nashville: Broadman Press, 1986.

National Black Sisters' Conference. *Tell It Like It Is: A Black Catholic Perspective on Christian Education*, ed. Eva Marie Lumas. Oakland, 1983.

Newsome, Timone. "Millennial Young Adults: Shapeshifters." *Church* Fall (2008 Center Section): 13–15.

Ogunjimi, Bayo and Abdul-RasheedNa' Allah.*Introduction to African Oral Literature and Performance.* Trenton, NJ: Africa World Press, Inc., 2005.

O' Keefe, Theresa."Mentoring Relationships in Ministry to Youth and Young Adults." Boston College, The Church in the 21st Century Center, recorded October 29, 2009. Accessed March 4, 2020. Accessed March 4, 2020, https://www.youtube.com/watch?v=Z0HdV-jSprU&t=74s.

———. "The Same But Different: The Culture in Which Our Adolescents Live." *Journal of Youth and Theology* 7, no. 2 (November 2008): 41–59.

Paul II, John. "The Apostolic Exhortation on Catechesis in Our Time *Catechesi Tradendae* (1979)." In *The Catechetical Documents: A Parish Resource*. Chicago: Liturgy Training Publications, 1996, 375–416.

Paul VI. "Dogmatic Constitution on Divine Revelation *Dei Verbum* (1965)." Accessed March 14, 2020). http://www.vatican.va/archive/hist_councils/ii_vat ican_council/documents/vat-ii_const_19651118_dei-verbum_en.html.

———. "The Apostolic Exhortation on Evangelization in the Modern World *Evangelii Nuntiandi*(1975)." In *The Catechetical Documents: A Parish Resource*. Chicago: Liturgy Training Publications, 1996, 157–199.

Pew Research Center. October 9, 2012. ""Nones" on the Rise." Accessed February 29, 2020. https://www.pewforum.org/2012/10/09/nones-on-the-rise/.

Piatt, Christian and Amy Piatt. *My Space to Sacred Space: God for a New Generation*. St. Louis: Chalice Press, 2007.

Raboteau, Albert J. *A Fire in the Bones: Reflections on African-American Religious History*. Boston: Beacon Press, 1995.

———. *Slave Religion: The "Invisible Institution" in the Antebellum South*. 2nd ed. Oxford, England: Oxford University Press, 2004.

Rambo, Shelly. *Resurrecting Wounds: Living in the Afterlife of Trauma*. Waco, TX: Baylor University Press, 2017.

Recinos, Harold J. "Transforming Ecclesiology: Hip-Hop Matters." In *In Our Own Voices: Latino/a Renditions of Theology*, ed. Benjamin Valentin, 155–170. Maryknoll, NY: Orbis Books, 2010.

Regan, Jane E. *Toward an Adult Church: A Vision of Faith Formation*. Chicago: Loyola Press, 2002.

Rivera, Raquel Z. *New York Ricans From the Hip Hop Zone*. New York: Palgrave Macmillan, 2003.

Roberts, J. Deotis. *Africentric Christianity: A Theological Appraisal for Ministry*. Valley Forge: Judson Press, 2000.

Scheub, Harold. *Story*. Madison: The University of Wisconsin Press, 1998.

Schreiter, Robert J. *The Ministry of Reconciliation: Spirituality and Strategies*. Maryknoll, NY: Orbis Books, 1998.

Schor, Juliet B. *Born To Buy: The Commercialized Child and the New Consumer Culture*. New York: Scribner, 2004.

Shaw, Susan M. *Storytelling in Religious Education*. Birmingham, AL: Religious Education Press, 1999.

Shimojima, Anne. "This Is Why I Tell It: The Value of Telling Stories." In *The Power of Story: Teaching through Storytelling*, eds. Rives Collins and Pamela Cooper. Long Grove, IL: Waveland Press, Inc., 2005.

Simpkinson, Charles H. and Anne Adamcewicz Simpkinson, eds. *Sacred Stories: A Celebration of the Power of Story to Transform and Heal*. San Francisco: HarperSanFrancisco, 1993.

Smedes, Lewis B. *The Art of Forgiving: When You Need to Forgive and Don't Know How*. Nashville, TN: Moorings, 1996.

Smith, Efrem and Phil Jackson. *The Hip-Hop Church*. Downers Grove: InterVarsity Press, 2005.

Strauss, William and Neil Howe. *Generations: The History of America's Future, 1584 to 2069*. New York: William Morrow, 1991.

StudyLib. "Generational Differences Chart." Accessed February 29, 2020. https://studylib.net/doc/8718132/generational-differences-chart.

Sullivan, Paula Farrell. *The Mystery of My Story: Autobiographical Writing for Personaland Spiritual Development*. Mahwah, NJ: Paulist Press, 1991.

Taylor, Paul and Scott Keeter, eds. "Millennials: A Portrait of Generation Next: Confident. Connected. Open to Change." *Pew Research Center*, February 21, 2010. Accessed March 2, 2020. www.pewresearch.org/millennials. This publication is part of a Pew Research Center report series that looks at the values, attitudes and experiences of America's next generation: The Millennials.

The Center for Generational Kinetics. "Generational Birth Years." Accessed February 29, 2020. https://genhq.com/generational_birth_years/.

U.S. Department of Health and Human Services Administration for Children and Families. Accessed March 6, 2020. https://www.acf.hhs.gov/trauma-toolkit/trauma-concept.

Watkins, Ralph C. "From Black Theology and Black Power to Afrocentric Theology and Hip Hop Power: And Extension and Socio-Re-Theological Conceptualization of Cone's Theology in Conversation with the Hip Hop Generation." *Black Theology: An International Journal*8, no. 3 (2010): 327–340.

Webster's Unabridged Dictionary of the English Language. Random House, Inc., 2001.

Westerhoff, III, John H. *Will Our Children Have Faith?* New York: The Seabury Press, 1976.

White, C. Vanessa. "Spirit and Story: An Emerging Model and Method of Theological Reflection."An emerging model at the Institute for Black Catholic Studies at Xavier University of LA, 2007.

Wimberly, Anne Streaty. *Nurturing Faith and Hope: Black Worship as a Model for Christian Education*. Cleveland: The Pilgrim Press, 2004.

———. *Soul Stories: African American Christian Education*. Nashville: Abingdon Press, 2005.

Wimberly, Edward P. *African American Pastoral Care*. Rev. ed. Nashville: Abingdon Press, 2008.

———. *Moving From Shame to Self-Worth: Preaching and Pastoral Care*. Nashville: Abingdon Press, 1999.

World Health Organization. "Naming the Coronavirus Disease (COVID-19) and the Virus that Causes It." Accessed March 19, 2020. https://www.who.int/emergencies/diseases/novel-coronavirus-2019/technical-guidance/naming-the-coronavirus-disease-(covid-2019)-and-the-virus-that-causes-it.

Wuthnow, Robert. *After the Baby Boomers: How Twenty- and Thirty-Somethings Are Shaping the Future of American Religion*. Princeton, NJ: Princeton University Press, 2010.

William S. Schmidt. "Theological and Spiritual Resources for Trauma." Unpublished Paper Dated February 12, 2018 and shared with the author during an in-person interview September 26, 2018

Index

Page references for figures are italicized.

About the Author

dr. timone a davis* is a cradle Catholic who was a "pewster" until she discovered that the uselessness of the Church was because she wasn't giving anything of herself. After committing to getting involved, her life changed. Her first ministry was with the RCIA, where she not only welcomed others into the Church but also revitalized her own spirituality.

In 2012 timone co-founded PEACE centered WHOLENESS, a clinical counseling and spiritual companioning endeavor.

timone's dynamic energy and deep spirituality enhance her brand of teaching that engages one's spirit through the use of storytelling. No matter the occasion, timone's mission is to help others open their hearts and minds to the soul-saving power of God's Grace, Love, and Mercy.

---

* dr. timone davis uses lower case letters in the spelling of her name to indicate her willingness to embody the creedal assertion in John 3:30 in her everyday living.